MANAGING THE MONKEY!

MANAGING THE MONKEY!

How to defuse the conflicts that can
lead to violence in the workplace

* * *

Mark Dawes with **Denise Winn**

Managing the Monkey!

The Therapist Ltd.
The Barn, Church Farm, Chalvington, Hailsham,
East Sussex BN27 3TD, United Kingdom

Printed in Great Britain by Cromwell Press, Trowbridge, Wiltshire.

ISBN 1 899398 02 3

MANAGING THE MONKEY!

CONTENTS

ABOUT THIS BOOK

THIS BOOK is based on my years of experience in defusing potentially violent situations at work and of teaching others how to do so. Later chapters explain in detail what to do to reduce the risk of ending up involved in a violent incident. However, that is not all that it is important to know.

Earlier in the book, in chapters 2 and 3, I explain in some depth the reasons that confrontation so often ends in violence. Included in this are the environments and cultures in which employees work. An understanding of this is vital because, while it may not be in an employee's power to change their working conditions, information provides ammunition to press for change and will also help individuals see how the *impact* of their working conditions may in turn affect their own behaviour.

In chapter 4 I take the reader through the legal responsibilities of employers, which are not yet being fully honoured, and the legal implications of employees' own actions, if they themselves use force to resolve conflict.

Chapter 5 explains the crucial effects of our biology upon our actions. I put the consequences of all this together in chapters 6, 7 and 8, where I explore a range of confrontational encounters which can lead to violence and injury and use them to illustrate how situations of such types can be handled with least risk to everyone involved. The book ends with a brief look at the future.

I have written this book because I would like our work environments to become far safer places in which to earn our livings. I hope you find it helpful.

Mark Dawes
February 1999, London

"All cruelty springs from weakness."

Seneca (4 B.C. – A.D. 65)

1 – Violence at work

IT SEEMS to happen with shocking regularity now – although the more it happens, the less we end up shocked by it. The drunk, badly cut from a fall and deposited by the police in a busy accident and emergency department, turns vicious with the very people who are trying to help him. The man at the doctor's surgery, feeling ill, upset and fed up with waiting in a queue to see his GP, when it's long past his appointment time, suddenly loses it and takes out his frustration on one of the reception staff, with her paperweight; an addict, angry not to get the drug supply he is after, attacks the GP who has withheld the prescription – or else he mugs another doctor or even a nurse getting out of a car in some residential street, hoping to find drugs in their bag.

The store manager hurt when trying to stop a shoplifter, the teacher assaulted and permanently crippled by the disruptive pupil she is trying to quieten, the air hostess hit with a bottle by a passenger, the housing department official punched and kicked by an irate and frustrated local resident – the list of scenarios in which people are nowadays attacked and injured when trying to do their jobs is, sadly, endless.

At last, however, industries and organisations whose employees have to deal with the public are starting to recognise violence at work as the enormous problem which it has become. Many companies are trying to find ways to deal with these growing difficulties, or at least realising they are going to have to – new legislation making them unequivocally legally responsible for the wellbeing of their staff in the workplace is finally forcing their hands (more of that in chapter 4). The problem is that, while all have emergency plans for eventualities such as fire, bomb threats and product contamination, few yet have effective strategies for dealing with potentially violent situations which, for most people who deal with the public, occur a lot more frequently than fires and bombs. That's of little comfort to their staff, who may find themselves risking their personal safety – and consequently their sanity – every day.

Let's look at the NHS, as an example. We all know that nurses are now regularly victims of violence. In fact, a staggering one in three nurses has suffered violence, according to a survey by the Health and Safety Executive, published in December 1997. This, compared with the one in four policemen and security officers who is a victim of violence, made nursing the most dangerous profession in Britain, it was pointed out at the time. Around the same time another survey, reported on the BBC's *Here and Now* programme, found that nearly half of nurses working in accident and emergency departments had been physically assaulted by patients and 96 per cent had suffered verbal abuse. A nursing sister at a London teaching hospital was quoted in the *Evening Standard* as saying that verbal abuse was worse than the fear of physical violence: "Day in, day out we have people swearing at us, being verbally aggressive and it becomes very demoralising".

The powers that be, at the top of the NHS, were not ignoring this dire situation. In summer 1997 Alan Langlands, the Chief Executive of the NHS Executive, wrote to the chief executives and chairmen of all NHS trusts, health authorities and special health authorities, alerting them to the findings of a National Audit Office report that accidents (of all kinds) in NHS hospitals were costing over £100 million a year. "Ensuring a safe and healthy environment for both staff and patients is an important management task and should be a priority for every NHS employer," Alan Langlands wrote.

In the attached Health Service Guidelines on NHS health and safety issues[1], it was emphasised that NHS employers must ensure that all staff were given appropriate health and safety training both when first recruited and when exposed to new or increased risks. Training was not only to cover issues such as good hygiene and safely controlling substances hazardous to health but also violence. Further, the need for refresher/update training was stressed "because an employee's competence will decline if skills and knowledge are not used regularly". Staff, advised the Guidelines, should be trained how to avoid or defuse potentially violent situations and how to respond appropriately to incidents of violence. They should also be offered support and counselling if subjected to violent attacks.

Fine words and laudable and sensible aims. But where are we now, over one year on, as regards training and handling of violence in NHS hospitals?

The issue of the *Nursing Times,* published on October 28, 1998, launched a Stamp Out Violence Campaign after finding from a poll of almost 1000 nurses that *one in two* nurses had been physically attacked in the previous 12 months. Forty seven per cent had been punched or slapped and 85 per cent had been verbally abused in the same period. Over a third said that slapping, punching and spitting were frequent and two thirds said swearing and shouting happened frequently. Other attacks included being lunged at with a knife, being confronted by a man wielding an iron bar, and having a finger pulled back aggressively.

In accident and emergency departments increasingly it is not drunks but patients and their relatives, frustrated by the long hours of waiting, who turn to physical and violent abuse. The *Nursing Times* poll found that almost half of those who verbally abused nurses were patients' relatives.

Nearly three quarters of nurses said they felt vulnerable to violence at work, with many saying, incredibly, that they felt safer walking alone down a dark street than in their hospitals a third even felt at risk when off duty. Eighty-one per cent thought physical and verbal aggression was more common than when they began their careers; the rest thought it was about the same. No one, of course, thought violence had decreased since they had started nursing.

Particularly horrifying, in the light of the Health Service Guidelines on health and safety which were supposed to have been given such priority more than a year before, were the findings that NHS trusts are largely *not* doing a lot to protect staff or help staff protect themselves. Only just over half had a policy on handling aggression. Seventy per cent of nurses had had no training in areas such as aggression management, risk assessment and control and restraint. Most trusts had incident reporting procedures but almost half were not viewed as providing clear information to staff. Over half of nurses said their working environment was poor in terms of simple safety factors such as good lighting and nearly three quarters were offered no safe transport when working unsocial late shifts. Finally, nearly two thirds of trusts offered no staff support, such as a violence helpline, in the event of violence.

This is very shocking stuff and letters published in the same issue of the *Nursing Times* only add to the horror. One nurse described an incident in which a patient who claimed to have taken an overdose ran at a doctor with a knife. The doctor escaped; the nursing staff were trapped. Even the security officers who were summoned kept well away from the man as he brandished the knife. Fortunately, in this instance, he suddenly just put it down of his own accord and no one was hurt. But it was left to the nurse to escort the patient back to his cubicle and to search him. His bag contained a broken light bulb and other weapons. "When the hospital managers were informed of the incident, not one of them came to see whether staff were all right," she wrote. "All of us had to continue to work. ... It is the nursing staff that have to carry on, no matter what. Eventually we were offered counselling but that took weeks to happen."

Nurses, of course, are not the only employee group who suffer particularly high levels of violence. According to a report[2] of a survey of crime suffered by retailers in 1996/7, one member of shop staff is assaulted or intimidated *every minute* in a typical shopping day and tackling shop thieves is the cause of 54 per cent of violent physical attacks on staff. Over 13,000 staff were the victims of violence in this period and 177,000 were subjected to threats of violence and to verbal abuse. "Overall, in 1996/97 the incidence of violence against staff showed a disturbing rise of 44 per cent ..." commented the compilers of the British Retail Consortium Retail Crime Survey.

Violent incidents on airlines have recently been making the news, with the number of attacks having increased dramatically over the last three years and with swearing and unpleasantness from passengers considered a normal hazard of daily work for airline staff. Recorded incidence of violence while flying has risen 400 per cent since 1995. In 1997 British Airways recorded more than 260 'air rage' incidents, with air hostesses having to handle both drunken and sexual assaults. (British Airways introduced restraint training for its 14,500 cabin crew three years ago but at the time considered it purely a precautionary measure.) The crews at Delta Air Lines suffer 100 physical and verbal assaults a month.

I could reel off figures for numerous groups of workers. Social workers, police officers, prison officers, utility company employees and many others are all facing unacceptably high risks but with inadequate training or refresher training to deal with it. But I think I've made the point.

Not only is the cost enormously high in human terms but the hidden costs to companies are astronomical too, with the knock on effect this has for the economy and jobs. Every year about 1.1 million employed people in the UK sustain a workplace injury. In 1990, 750,000 employees had to take time off for ill health caused or made worse by their work, resulting in a loss of over 30 million working days and a cost to industry of almost £70 million. The overall cost to employers of work accidents and work related ill health (including that caused by violent attack) is estimated to be between £4,000 million and £9,000 million every year!

It is telephone number stuff, this. Telescoping it down a little, the Health and Safety Executive carried out a survey[3] which showed that, on average, accidents cost each hospital about £397,000 a year (equivalent to five per cent of a hospital's running costs). Overall, £191 million was paid out last year on temporary nurse fees and £380 million on overtime, to cover for the loss of regular staff through accidents. The NHS also spent £41 million on job adverts – very many health service staff who are injured in violent attacks do not go back to their jobs.

For every £1 of insured costs, companies lose between £8 and £36 in uninsured costs. Legal expenses, fines, the effects of bad publicity, the cost of job advertisements, overtime costs, etc, are not reclaimable. And there are the other uninsurable costs such as loss of business image, customer satisfaction, employee morale, goodwill and productivity.

Why now?

Violence at work is not a new phenomenon for those whose work requires them to be in contact with the public. But why is it escalating now? Why do we hear more now of violence within services where little was heard before – on the airlines, for instance, and in schools? One nurse who wrote in the *Nursing Times* issue that launched their Stamp Out Violence Campaign said that, in her long experience of working in an accident and emergency department, people nowadays seemed to her increasingly selfish and less tolerant of any kind of authority. She has a strong point. Aviation consultancy Dahlberg and Associates, which investigated causes in violent incidents logged by one American airline carrier over a six month period, also blamed changes in society's views on technology and authority for the increase in violence. That, it would seem, may be one reason why the fists actually fly. There isn't the respect left for others to hold them back.

But surely something else has to explain why things reach such a pitch in the first place. Prime candidate appears to be that much over-used (and mis-used) word, stress. We are constantly told that stress is a major cause of ill health and ill-advised actions. Dahlberg and Associates cited stresses related to mass travel as a cause of air rage. Farrol Kahn, director of the Aviation Health Institute, also puts most passenger misbehaviour down to stress. Overcrowding, queuing and waiting in the terminal building raise adrenaline levels, only to be followed by being cramped and cooped up for hours on the aircraft. It may take just one more annoyance for some to lose their cool and blow their top.

A study published in 1997 by NOP Consumer Research found that the 'stress' of modern life has made 90 per cent of the population much more angry than they were 10 years ago. One thousand men and women were interviewed. Women were found to be even more likely to lose their cool than men, with seven out of 10 expecting to become angry in stressful situations. Half of those surveyed had also been on the receiving end of some one else's ire. The situations that respondents cited as most stressful were being made to wait on the phone 'on hold'

(44 per cent found this a rage inducer), being irritated by other drivers on the road (42 per cent), public transport, supermarket check-outs and crowds. Parents of young children were more likely to be quick to anger than childless people. Ten per cent of those interviewed admitted to getting angry at least once every day.

A stress management expert quoted in the *Daily Mail*'s report of the survey said "the problem was not that people had grown angrier in themselves but that nowadays they exposed themselves to more stressful situations than ever before".

Stress itself is not what is harmful (as I shall explain in the next chapter). However, increasingly we are put into situations where we have little control, often because of the effects of cost cutting to increase competitiveness or because of lack of money. So there are more seats crammed on to airlines and the food is poorer. So there are fewer staff dealing with emergencies in hospital casualty departments and patients have to wait longer. And so on down the line. That is when stress is harmful and the result is danger for those, unconnected with the commercial decisions, who have to work with its effects – the quickly irate 'customer'.

But there is another commercial decision which, I believe, is accounting for much of the escalation in violence. It is companies' current mission to put 'customers first' and I'm going to look at the significance of that in the next chapter.

1   NHS Health and Safety Issues (1997). *Health Service Guidelines*, HSG (97) 6, 13 June.
2   *Retail crime costs: survey 1996/7.* British Retail Consortium. February 1998.
3   Health and Safety Executive (1997). The *Costs of Accidents at Work*. HSE Books.

2 – Customers should come second

"We guarantee to provide you with the very best of service at the very cheapest of prices." "If your washing machine/ television/ dishwasher breaks down, we'll have it mended within two hours." "Call us to deliver your parcel and we'll have it there before midday." "If we aren't there within 40 minutes, you can have your money back." "An appointment guaranteed to be offered within two days."

You know the sort of thing. It's what a host of companies, big, small and tiny (one boss and an assistant) now offer as a way of ensuring that you will consider them trustworthy and therefore give them your custom. They make cast iron promises because they know that that is what customers want – certainty that their problem or need is going to be given the priority it deserves. None of that wishy-washy politician stuff when you hedge your bets and avoid getting talked into a corner. No, be specific and spell out what's on offer.

In theory it is an excellent idea. Everyone knows what to expect. Everyone knows what's to be delivered. It's excellent for everyone except the company employee who has to do the delivering.

Suppose the guarantee made by a car breakdown service is that, if there is a problem, a mechanic will be on the site working on the problem within three quarters of an hour. A call comes in to the company for immediate help. A man's car won't start and he has somewhere urgent to get to. The young woman on the switchboard checks which mechanics are doing what and finds that Mick Mendit is the nearest to the new problem area. He is working on a job on the other side of the town, not too far away, by the look of the map, says the switchboard operator. Mick is a bit reluctant to take the new job on because he knows he won't be finished his present job

9

for at least another 10 minutes. But it seems there is no one else in a better position than he is.

It is another 15 minutes before he is ready to leave. He gets into his car, checks his street map and groans. There is no way to the road where the next client lives except by going through the heaviest area for traffic. It is 5pm on a Friday night. The roads are going to be a nightmare.

As he sits in an enormous traffic jam, he gets more and more frustrated and stressed. By the time he reaches the house he is 20 minutes late and almost at the end of his tether. So is the man with the broken down car. Tempers are very ready to flare. So before they even meet, they've already got another problem to overcome besides the fault with the car.

Mission statements and customer charters are being pelted out from companies of all sizes like sweets from a machine. The companies think it is good for business. But in many cases it is all at the expense of staff.

Mick can't control the traffic. He also can't rush the job he was working on just because the company has no one more conveniently placed to send to the next job. So the company's guarantee is entirely unrealistic. Either staff can only meet unrealistic imposed deadlines by becoming stressed and overworked, or they fail to meet them because it is a simple physical impossibility. Either way the service they finally offer to the customers concerned is unlikely to be service with a smile.

Mission statements and customer charters of these kinds – the kinds that aren't thought through and backed up with sufficient numbers of staff – can lead to inflexible and deadening working environments with little room for innovation or entrepreneurial flair from staff. In such environments there is often an authoritarian hierarchical system of accountability which leaves staff feeling they are just a minuscule part of a rigidly controlled production system aimed at achieving the corporate vision.

Policies which take away the initiative from staff often leave them the most exposed to aggression from the very public they are supposed to be serving. If you have been sitting on a train stuck in the middle of the countryside, fuming because it hasn't moved for the last half hour, wondering what on earth is going on and why no one is telling you anything, you might be inclined to go and have a strong word with the train driver or the man at the ticket barrier when you finally arrive. Are you going to feel better if he gives you a sheet of paper from Superwheels, 'the railway for the future', apologising for any delay and inviting you to write to the customer care department if you have any complaint? It is quite likely that, for a few passengers at least, that sheet of paper will be like a red rag to a bull, the final indignity after a highly frustrating journey. But all the rail worker can do is shrug and tell them that they'll have to write to the company, if they have any problem with the system. And if that isn't quite good enough for some, tempers may end up fraying on all sides, with violence not an entirely unforeseeable outcome.

All a company is doing, when it invites dissatisfied customers to write in with complaints, is admitting that it cannot do the job it promised to do. And in forcing workers to toe the company line and follow policy ("hand out the sheets and say nothing incriminating"), they are disempowering them from actually doing something *at the time* to deal with the situation or at least improve it.

Of course not all companies are like this. An increasing number have taken to heart the Investors in People scheme, realising that their workforce is their most valuable resource and that they need to make their workers feel suitably valued. Some organisations talk about the 'internal customer', meaning all other employees that staff work with, and try to encourage them to treat those employees with the same respect they hope that they accord their external customers. But for all those companies that are investing in people, there are still a host more where only lip service is paid to the idea or where the word doesn't even pass company lips. And even companies who *are* trying to invest in people may still fall foul of the human consequences of cost-cutting exercises.

To go back to the example of the delayed train, it is quite common that there is no announcement explaining what is happening. Yet there are constant announcements when it is simply a case of supplying uncontentious information, such as where the train will stop next and where the buffet is situated. So why the silence? Probably for the same reason that the ticket collector or conductor is often reluctant to walk through the train to speak to the passengers in person. They don't want to provoke people's anger when they haven't got anything good to report or any power to take the initiative themselves. Yet walking through the train is exactly the thing to do because it will dissipate anger. Which would you rather? To sit on the train wondering what is happening and when it might start again, seething about missed appointments or missed dinners? Or to see a company representative walking firmly through the carriages saying something like, "I'm terribly sorry, we've been unavoidably delayed. I do have a mobile phone here, if anyone needs to make a call."

If employees can say or do something, however minor, that they think may alleviate the situation, they experience both satisfaction and a sense of achievement. They are motivated to do their job because they can make a difference, and it isn't a small one. Ironically enough, customers are happier too. It is these outcomes that are lost when employees are forced to stay 'on message'.

Smile please

Another way that companies may do a disservice to employees is through insistence on making them act in an unnatural way. Certain major service industries, for instance, issue a written code which requires staff to be friendly, warm and approachable at all times – and to smile. We all know that staff at McDonald's fast food outlets are meant to smile at every customer and wish them a nice day. This works well in America, where of course McDonald's originated. It is common in a great many restaurants in America for waiting staff to greet you with an enormous smile, instantly offer you a drink and genuinely wish you a nice day when you leave. It seems to go with the culture. But it doesn't import too well. In Britain, staff aren't always so keen to dress up in their McDonald's uniforms and wish every customer a nice day, an expression which never would have crossed their minds in any other circumstances. When the words emerge from their lips, they are probably really saying: "I feel stupid and embarrassed. Take your burger and go away, so I don't have to feel so stupid any more." Being approachable and friendly is one thing. But trotting out the same alien expression is quite another. It can, in effect, lead to contempt of the customer – the very last thing the company had in mind – because of the resentment caused by having to speak to them in this way.

Disneyland also have a written code about niceness. Staff are meant to produce self esteem-enhancing emotions, so that guests feel good. Something similar seems to operate in the Disney shops that sell Disney products. My wife, as well as many of her friends, she says, dislikes going into the Disney shop in a large shopping centre near us because there is always someone outside smiling, trying to engage with her. "Hi, there! Are you having a good day?" "Bye now, come back soon, now, won't you?" She'll do anything to avoid the speaker's eye, wishing to remain with her own thoughts and preoccupations, rather than feel invaded by someone else's patently phoney interest in her and have to put on a fake smile herself and chat back. So how does the poor staff person feel, as they send out all this forced bonhomie into the ether and watch customers slink by, doing anything to avoid them? Not good, I imagine, about themselves or the company – unless they are out of work actors.

In *Mapping the Mind*,[1] Rita Carter explains that social smiles are quite distinct from genuine smiles of pleasure. They are brought about by different sets of facial muscles which are each controlled by completely separate brain circuits. The genuine smile, the type that happens when we see someone we like or love, comes from the unconscious brain and is not under our control. The social smile comes from the conscious cortex and can be summoned at will. It also disappears extremely quickly and leaves no trace, whereas the true smile fades more slowly. We all know that a true smile involves the eyes – tiny muscles around the eye sockets contract – but the social smile does not. What is the point of social smiles? Carter says they are one of a number of expressions which "provide us with a formidable battery of tools for easing social intercourse." Social smiles "have a very specific role: they allow us to lie about our inner feelings. Other animals do not have this dubious ability because their facial expressions are out of their control."

It is true that, if you see someone smile, it may make you smile in turn. Carter cites experiments in which tiny sensors were attached to people's smile muscles. Seeing other smiling faces triggered automatic mimicking of the smile, although it was often imperceptible to an onlooker. But the tiny twitch of the smile muscles, whether visible to others or not, could be sufficient to trigger a feedback mechanism that leads the brain to experience momentary pleasure. That, of course, is the thinking behind the company smile policies.

But it appears unlikely that the smile effect keeps the smiler happy. Psychologist Sandi Mann undertook some research at the University of Salford and found that people who mask their feelings at work may be putting their health at risk. Pretending to be enthusiastic and friendly and interested when you aren't causes huge amounts of stress and can raise the risks of heart disease, she found.

It isn't just American companies which require staff to be customer friendly. And, of course, it is no bad thing to be customer friendly. The damage occurs when staff themselves do not feel valued by the company. It is difficult to be warm and expansive and act as an ambassador for a company which an employee experiences as demanding and disrespectful.

Feeling low

If employees feel they are just part of a production system, with few if any chances to do their job in their own way, even when initiative seems called for, they are likely to end up feeling isolated, demotivated and lacking in self worth and self esteem.

Business Blueprints, a retail marketing consultancy carried out a survey of 500 'frontline' workers. Forty per cent of workers in fast food outlets and 17 per cent of those working in shops said they had taken their jobs only because they were the only ones they could get. Over 90 per cent said they received no respect in their jobs. Overall, retailing was viewed as an industry requiring few if any qualifications and offering little or no training and no recognition, rewards or prospects. As a result, employees were not motivated to do their jobs well and were, in fact, completely uninterested in them, despite exhortations from the company, in the form of mission statements and corporate aims, to give good service to the customer.

According to the report by Business Blueprints, the lack of respect which the workers felt was accorded to them was in turn passed on to the customer. Rather than be treated disrespectfully by the customer, as they tended

15

to expect, they preferred to 'get in first' by being offhand and not very helpful. They were indifferent to customers' needs because they felt their company was indifferent to their own. Stephen Logue, chief executive of Business Blueprints and author of the report, said that highly motivated managers failed to recognise employees' feelings of worthlessness.

The lower someone's self esteem and self confidence, the higher their anxiety levels. And the higher the anxiety, the higher the risks of anger and hostility, bubbling beneath the surface and ready, at some trigger moment, to burst out.

It should be well known to those charged with employees' safety that violence doesn't come out of the blue or only on occasions when the perpetrator is drunk, drugged or maddened, as per popular misconception. Violent reactions are all too often a product of the ambience or work culture that employees find themselves in. Where communication is poor and pressure is severe, the risks of violence escalate.

I can give you a clear example. Because psychiatric nurses are so often at risk at work, researchers Jonathan Warren and Alan Beadsmoore reviewed a number of studies which looked at the characteristics of violent and peaceful wards. They wrote in the Nursing Times:[2] "Typically violent wards are characterised by an atmosphere of distrust with limited and often hostile communication between staff and patients.

"Most meetings and activities were occasional and took place at unscheduled times. Staff responsibilities were not clearly defined and patients were not sure who to approach about their problems and requests.

"Staff morale was low and staff communication and support was poor. Staff constantly complained about their workload, patients, hospital and psychiatrists.

"In contrast, peaceful wards had regular meetings and activities that were scheduled and followed closely.

Everybody was aware of what was happening and when. Staff responsibilities were clearly defined and staff functioned in a coordinated fashion. The patients knew who was responsible for what and teamwork predominated."[3,4]

The more staff can participate and have a say in the way their work is done, the healthier – mentally and physically – the workforce. Researchers from University College London Medical School followed over 10,000 London-based male and female civil servants for five years. They found that those who were given at least an area of control over their own jobs by their bosses were at lower risk of heart disease. (And, as Professor Michael Marmot, professor of epidemiology and public health at University College London, pointed out: "Most people will have a boss, however high up they are".) For men there was a 50 per cent higher risk of new illness in those who had low job control – defined as not having a choice in what they did, what speed they did it at and who they worked with. Women were at slightly lower risk but low job control was still a significant factor in whether they fell ill or not. As Professor Marmot commented to the *Daily Mail*: "Job control is not something you can grab for yourself. It's to do with the way the job is structured."

One of the individual risk factors for heart disease is hostility – just the sort of emotion that builds up when you feel trapped, resentful and worthless.

Sabotage

It is human nature to want to fight back when individuals feel they are not respected or valued. One means to which some employees may resort is the covert expression of anger through sabotage of management's plans. I saw this ploy often when I was in the prison service. A prison governor might, for instance, tell one of the prison officers on A wing that he wants them to institute a sports programme for inmates. It should take the form of an extra hour of physical exercise. "Good idea, sir," says the prison officer, "but we haven't got enough staff to be able to do it". The prison governor is of the old school. "That's an order, Bloggs." "Yes, sir," says the prison officer. He doesn't like that and nor do his colleagues, but they have to obey.

So the prison officers carry out the order. However, they do it in such a way that it disrupts the running of other aspects of the prison. They take the inmates to the gym during the period when the inmates were due to make their weekly visit to the canteen.

Now the weekly visit to the canteen means a lot to the men on A wing. They look forward to buying their smokes and chocolate bars and bits and pieces. When they arrive back on the wing and ask when they are going to the canteen, they are outraged when they learn that they have missed their chance to go down. "Why can't we go now?" "Can't go now. The other wings are going down. You'll have to wait till next week," say the prisoner officers.

That alone is nearly grounds for a riot. But someone is sensible and insists on going to the prison governor to complain. When the governor finds himself on the receiving end of all this pent up anger, he quickly calls the prison officers on A wing and tells them to take the inmates to the canteen anyway. It was, after all, never his intention that the extra physical education sessions should be seen as a punishment.

So the prison officers obey the order: but grudgingly. They take the inmates down to the canteen and they line up. But then D wing is brought down and the prison officers say, "we are supposed to be behind C wing." So the A wing officers say, "no problem, mate, you go ahead. We'll queue after you." And then the same thing happens with E wing and so on. By the time the inmates get to the counter, they are boiling with anger again and that soon gets back to the prison governor in a highly heated form. The governor doesn't like being the bad guy, especially when he was doing his best. "Why didn't you take them straight to the front of the queue?" he blusters down the phone. "Oh, awfully sorry, sir," says the prison officers' representative with one of those smiles that aren't genuine. "We didn't think we could do *that,* sir. It's rude."

And so we have it. The staff are busy focusing on getting the better of each other instead of providing a good service for the inmates. This kind of climate generated at the inmates' expense is one in which violence could erupt at any second.

Misunderstandings

Sometimes, far from trying to sabotage what are perceived as their bosses' more unrealistic demands, employees may put themselves in danger because of a misunderstanding of what is expected of them or a fear of being viewed as weak by their peers. To return to the prison service for a moment: prison officers must all be trained in control and restraint techniques, to enable them to safely restrain a prisoner who is becoming violent. However training in these techniques must be updated regularly, otherwise a prison officer is classed in law as not competent to use them. Horrifying as it sounds, only 40 per cent of prison officers are up to date with control and restraint training. That means over half are not capable, in law, of helping restrain a prisoner safely. Yet, in the event of an incident, many of those officers will indeed come to the aid of their colleagues. Why? They may fear that, unofficially, they will be held to account by their superiors if they back off. They fear being seen, both by management and their mates, as having let their colleagues down. Also, if they are undermanned, overworked and resentful, they will be stressed, jumpy and more ready to overreact. Any pent up anger may more easily be vented against a prisoner who is 'asking for it' than against management. And so more injuries occur.

Similarly, the shop security man or the assistant store

manager, mindful of edicts that the company is losing too much money because of stolen stock, may feel it encumbent on himself to tackle the shoplifter making off with a bottle of whisky – and who happens to have a knife. His fear of being chastised for losing stock overrides his memory of being told that employees must put safety before property. No one is ever expected to risk their own life to save an employer's property. But the messages that employees 'hear' are much more mixed than that.

Conversely, however, employees may feel that on occasions when they do give their best to save property or avert violence, they are the ones who end up being investigated. Even when prison officers are up to date on their control and restraint techniques training, for instance, there is always a risk that someone may get hurt, however competent the officers. A prisoner may complain that he was assaulted or that excessive force was used. It is certainly true that that is sometimes the case but more often the complaints are false. However, once the complaint is made, the prison officer will, rightly, be investigated for his role in the event. In badly run prisons, the attention may suddenly shift away *completely* from the prisoner's possible role in the event and, if the prison officer is found guilty, he will be disciplined or sacked.

It is as hard for a prison officer to prove that he didn't use excessive force as it is for a prisoner to prove that he did. But if the culture is one where the prison officer feels the prisoner is believed and 'valued' more than himself, he is not going to want to put himself in the frontline again.

Ironically prison officers may be more fearful of being investigated or disciplined than they are of being hurt in an attack. But the net effect is the same. When the next incident occurs and colleagues call for assistance, they are likely to hang back. "It's management's problem, not mine. Last time I tried to solve it, I got a blasting. So *they* can deal with it this time." But then they may be reviled by colleagues for not helping out. So, it's damned if they do and damned if they don't, which hardly breeds a constructive attitude in the workplace.

It isn't only those with high risk jobs like prison officers or the police who may be more fearful of discipline than violence. People in more peaceable employment don't want to face discipline or lose their jobs, so they don't want to get it wrong, when dealing with customers or patients. If something isn't working or someone has a complaint, they may think that, if they don't make a decision or if they stick to the book, they can't get it wrong – and the effect is that they opt out of customer relations altogether. This is the 'It's not my fault, I didn't make the rules' immovable type of approach, where no practical assistance of any kind is offered, which is guaranteed to rouse customers and patients to fury. This can be particularly dangerous if the staff member becomes seen as a faceless, almost inhuman, representative of the system and therefore fair game for the latter to vent their aggression upon.

The outcome of anger

People exposed to violence are most likely to leave that industry, if they are able to get a different type of job. If they can't get another job or can't afford to take a lesser paying job, they may stay with the company but start taking more and more time off sick. Some of that sickness might be feigned. Much of it will be stress-related. We all need some stress in order to function (more of that in the next chapter). Stress is only a problem when people are aroused by situations they are unable to act upon, thus unable to eliminate or at least reduce the stress. The build up of stress has been linked with a whole variety of conditions in humans, including heart disease, strokes, migraine, indigestion, stomach ulcers, irritable bowel syndrome, cancer, diabetes, skin conditions and nervous breakdowns.

That is what can happen in the kind of work environments and cultures I have been describing where lack of support and respect leaves people feeling ineffectual, demoralised and unable to use their initiative. And, of course, when people are off sick, there are even fewer staff left to cope with the demands that may have been too much to cope with in the first place.

It takes two

When people feel unsupported in their work or that unrealistic demands are being made of them, the risk of aggression always rises. It usually takes two people to make an episode violent. A man may brandish a knife or jump up and down swearing but it is how those facing him react that will decide whether the incident ends in violence or not. If an individual is highly stressed because of the kinds of problems in the workplace I have been discussing so far, they are going to reach flashpoint a lot earlier than they would have if they worked in a supportive, motivating and satisfying environment. They may just react in a way which fans the flames instead of dampening them. Sometimes they do it unintentionally. Other times it may be deliberate, even if unconscious. We may welcome a reason to let our bottled up anger and resentment go. The result may be inappropriate levels of force, but more of that in chapter 4.

Whether staff are off sick long term with stress-related illnesses or recovering from violent assaults, the outcome for the employer is the same. Fewer people to provide the standards of customer care that are deemed so important in mission statements, corporate aims and customer charters, and which cause a good proportion of the problems in the first place.

Yet it wouldn't have to be like that, if companies put *employees* first.

1   Carter, R (1998) *Mapping the Mind.* Weidenfeld and Nicolson, London.
2   Warren, J and Beadsmoore, A (1997). Preventing violence on mental health wards. *Nursing Times*, 93, 34, 47-48.
3   Katz, P and Kirkland F (1990). Violence and social structure on mental health wards. *Psychiatry*, 156, 846-852.
4   Stanton, A and Schwartz, M (1954). *The Mental Hospital.* Tavistock, London.

CHAPTER 3   EMPLOYEES FIRST

IT IS MY firm belief that managements would provide a far better service if they put the interests of their employees before those of their customers.

It is common sense when you think about it. We all know how to be nice. For most of us it is natural to want to be nice. We want to help other people, smile, be polite. And we are most likely to be helpful and pleasant if our experience is that most people are nice to *us*. Even at the simplest levels, little kindnesses breed kindnesses and care.

I remember laughing once at a monologue by brilliant Irish comedian Dave Allan in which he was talking about driving. He described how he might be going along the main road and see someone who wanted to turn out of a side road. If he was feeling in a good and expansive mood, he would motion the driver to move out in front of him. And the effect, of course, was that he felt good about himself. But then the driver in front, responding to the consideration Allan had shown him, in turn let another driver out in front of him. And then that driver, wishing to respond in kind for the consideration shown to him, also let in another driver. And so on, and so on. The end result, of course, deliberately exaggerated, was that Allan was left fuming and miles back in the traffic queue because everyone else was getting in ahead of him, all because of his original generosity. His humorous message was that what started out as his road courtesy ended up in virtual road rage. But we are amused by the story because we can identify: we instinctively understand that desire to reciprocate a small act of thoughtfulness.

It is a trait that organisations – both large and small, even the 'one boss and one helper' variety – can usefully capitalise on. By treating staff well, involving them in decisions about how to do their jobs, acknowledging their efforts, recognising their successes and remunerating them adequately, staff are likely to be better equipped, emotionally, mentally and physically, to offer their best to the public they serve. It all comes back to respect and value. If we feel valued and respected for the contributions we make in life, we are more likely to value and respect others.

The motivating factor

If you notice, in the paragraph above when I was writing about the ways organisations might best show their staff that they value their contribution, I put remuneration last. That's not because it is the least important. But it is certainly not necessarily the most important aspect of work for many people. Good pay does not make working for an authoritarian over-demanding company so sufficiently okay that we feel good about working there and able to pass that feel-good factor on to our customers and clients.

Many psychologists have looked at the enormous subject of what motivates human beings. One of the theories that became very popular as an explanation for what motivates people in the workplace is that developed by Abraham Maslow in 1954.[1]

Maslow proposed in his theory that human beings have special instinctive psychological needs, unique to our species, that go far beyond the physiological needs all animals share. He saw human needs in terms of 'hierarchies of prepotency': in other words, that we have a range of different needs and only when the more basic ones at the bottom of the hierarchy are met do we move on to concern ourselves with the next one up. He demonstrated his theory with a pyramid. At the bottom come the physiological needs – food, drink, air, sex (in terms of reproduction) and shelter. If these needs are not satisfied, an individual's energies will be directed almost totally towards survival. They won't be concerned with much else in the way of satisfaction.

Most people in our culture, and probably all people who have jobs, are fortunate not to have to worry too much about these. Once survival needs are met, an individual can move up to the next level of the hierarchy – safety needs. Here we would include the need for security, stability and some order and structure in one's life. Belonging and love needs become important, once security is assured. In this category Maslow was thinking of the need to be a part of a social group and the quality of one's relationships with important others. Next up the hierarchy he placed needs for esteem: having respect for oneself and being respected by others.

Finally, at the peak of one's functioning, comes self actualisation, which he defined as: "the desire to become more and more what one is, to become everything that one is capable of becoming". He thought that, unless a person could do what it was that they were best 'fitted' for, they would be restless, regardless of whether all other needs were met. Quite what self actualisation meant for individuals would vary enormously. One might want to be a wonderful mother, another might want to express athletic skills, another write, paint, make music or construct artefacts.

Later in life Maslow modified his theory, concluding that the need to reach each level in the hierarchy in turn was not rigid. Some people might find self esteem more important to them than belonging. A single parent might prefer to struggle to make ends meet rather than seek a full time job that would take him or her away from the children (thus putting love needs before those for security). And someone who is determined on self actualisation – making it as a writer, artist or athlete, for instance – might choose to go without sufficient food or clothing in order to devote their time or resources to furthering their ultimate goal. A hunger striker, of course, bargains his basic needs in order to achieve a higher goal. (Maslow, however, later reluctantly concluded that not everyone does strive for self actualisation, and that there is an innate tendency towards inertia in humans which it takes a lot of energy to want to overcome.)

Maslow's theory is only that, a theory. However it does focus us on the likely range of needs that individuals need met and it can still help employers understand more about what motivates their workers. For instance, providing good pay packets clearly isn't the be all and end all. Pay may be the overriding concern and cause of dissatisfaction if it is low. But, should it be increased, workers are likely then to seek more satisfaction from the work they do, more acknowledgement for doing it, a chance to advance and to do the job they are best fitted to do. Also, for many, satisfaction and esteem needs may be more (or just as) important than the wage packet. Nurses, for instance, are unlikely to enter the profession because they think it pays well, although it is certainly a source of dissatisfaction that it pays badly. Money is a benchmark for how people are valued in the workplace. But it often isn't the biggest motivator at work.

Well run companies and organisations take on board the variety of people's needs and aim to meet them because they know that, with a satisfied workforce, they are likely to have a more successful business or operation.

Security needs, as we can see, are pretty basic to Maslow's hierarchy. While we can see that it is possible to shift the order of some other elements in the hierarchy, putting esteem before relationships etc, it is very hard to be fulfilled in other needs if we don't feel safe. The person who feels vulnerable at work will lose self esteem, because fear erodes it. If fear and anxiety become pervasive, family relationships can suffer as well as work performance. We feel safe in groups. But if our own sense of security is compromised by the threat or experience of violence, and self esteem and self confidence suffer, we may find ourselves becoming more isolated, withdrawing from groups, and losing our sense of belonging with our colleagues.

Expectation

Some people give their best at work, others don't. I have already mentioned the research by Business Blueprints which found that 90 per cent of workers in retail felt they were accorded no respect for the jobs they did and that their work offered little recognition, rewards or prospects. As a result they were uninterested in their jobs or their customers.

How does such a situation develop? Other psychologists have looked at the effect of expectation on achievement motivation. Much of the original work in this area was done with children where it has been found that motivation in children is closely correlated with the expectations of their parents. For instance, parents whose children were highly motivated to achieve tended to *expect* their children to be successful in developmental tasks (such as buttoning coats or tying laces) at an early stage and were also more likely to reward them with kisses and cuddles.[2] In another experiment, children were blindfolded and asked to build a tower of bricks. Those children who were keenest to give the task their best shot had parents who set them high standards and who also praised them more for the efforts they made.[3] Importantly it is not rewarding a child for getting it right that seems to count but praising their efforts. In a recent study reported in *The Therapist*,[4] psychologists at Columbia University in New York gave children a test on which they were all able to achieve a high score. Half of the children were told how clever they were, the rest were praised for having worked really hard. Then all the children were invited to choose a second task, either one that they would know how to do or one that would be more challenging. Most of the children who were told they were clever opted for the familiar task while those who were praised for effort went for the challenge. The psychologists suggested that children designated 'clever' did not want to risk failing and therefore took the easy option while those who had been praised for trying hard wanted to try even harder. The researchers also found that 'clever' children, when they did make a mistake, tended to want to give up because they thought cleverness was a fixed trait, whereas the 'work hard' children thought working hard made the difference and one could always improve.

It is easy to see how all this can be extrapolated to the workplace. Employers who have expectations of their workforce and reward for effort, whether by acknowledgement, increasing responsibility, promotion, or pay, are more likely to have highly motivated workers. But people have to be able to make mistakes. It is all part of the learning curve and an important factor in motivation. And making mistakes is only likely to occur where workers are given the opportunity, where appropriate, to use their initiative.

The self fulfilling prophecy

An important aspect of the effects of expectation is what psychologists Rosenthal and Jacobsen termed the self fulfilling prophecy. Many researchers have performed similar experiments with different groups of people but the initial research was carried out in an American school. The children were given an IQ test and the teachers were told that the test was able to assess which children would be late developers and would be able to achieve well academically even though their school career had not started out too brilliantly. The researchers ensured that the teachers overheard a discussion in which they named a group of children (in fact picked at random) who were the ones who would suddenly put on an academic spurt.

One year later, the researchers tested the children again and found that the named at random children had all advanced quite significantly in their learning. The younger the child the more marked the improvement but the older the child the more lasting the effect. It appeared that the teachers had become far more encouraging of those children and successfully conveyed their higher expectations of them.[5]

Of course, all this can work in reverse as well. If someone is viewed as lazy, stupid, unable to take responsibility etc, it is quite likely that that will become the case as well. And then we are back with an unhappy, unmotivated – and at risk – workforce. I use the words 'at risk' for two reasons. People who are unhappy about their work ethos and environment are quicker to anger and quicker to get ill.

Learned helplessness

Also crucial to motivation is the perception that we can have a positive impact on what we do. We act or speak out and something good or better happens. But if we act and speak out and nothing beneficial happens, we may stop taking action at all. If rules are rigid, if our version of events is never taken into account, if there is no room for us to introduce our own ideas or try out improvements to the system, we may become apathetic and hopeless and this can be dangerous to health – both our own and the organisation's.

Being – or feeling – unable to act is what psychologist Martin Seligman and colleague Steven Maier termed 'learned helplessness' back in the late 1960s. Seligman and Maier discovered the phenomenon when they were testing a particular learning theory on dogs. The tests involved administering electric shocks to dogs which were strapped down and couldn't escape them. The dogs were later put into compartmentalised boxes from which they could escape by jumping over barriers. The researchers fully expected them to jump over the barriers when they gave the dogs shocks. But the dogs simply ran round the box for a short while trying to find a way out and then gave up and resigned themselves to the shocks, quietly whining.[6]

Whatever one may think of the ethics of such a painful experiment, Seligman found its outcome edifying. It seemed that the dogs were reacting to their previous experience of being totally unable to control what was happening to them. They couldn't escape the shocks when strapped down, so now they assumed they couldn't escape them in any environment. They had learned that their actions had no effect and they were helpless.

The researchers then tried some experiments with humans. Students who were subjected to the experience of being unable to turn off a loud unpleasant noise, whatever knobs on a machine they twiddled, didn't even try to control the noise on a different occasion, even when they could have done so. Others have tried similar experiments since. For instance, researchers gave students some puzzles, none of which was it possible to solve. The students weren't told this, of course, and struggled in vain to find solutions. When, on another occasion, they were given a series of puzzles which could be solved, they gave up far more quickly than other students who had not had to work on the impossible puzzles.[7] One can see this syndrome in the workplace. If employees are set the impossible task of delivering goods or completing repairs by a certain unrealistic time, they are likely to become demoralised and demotivated. Gradually, even when it is possible to achieve whatever the mission statement guarantees, they may feel the impossible is being asked of them and that it isn't worth even making the effort.

Seligman saw this same syndrome in people suffering from depression.[8] People who experience setbacks or losses over which they have no control may learn to think they can never have control, whatever the circumstances, that things will never turn out as they want them to and they may as well stop trying.

Consequently they suffer loss of motivation, lack of interest, self denigration and misery – all symptoms of depression. His suggestion was that therapy should concentrate on showing the depressed person that they *could* have an impact, by setting and then meeting small goals.

Of interest to many other investigators was the fact that the animals in Seligman's learned helplessness experiments very often became ill or more susceptible to disease. And that is what I'd like to look at next.

By any other name but stress

An enormous number of conditions have been attributed to what has now become quite a catch-all word – stress. I listed quite a number of them in the last chapter and I'll recap them here. Heart disease, strokes, migraine, indigestion, stomach ulcers, irritable bowel syndrome, cancer, diabetes, skin conditions and nervous breakdowns, among others, have all been linked with stress.

The most common symptoms arising from a build up of stress are any of the following: feeling short-tempered, feeling constantly on edge, loss of energy, lack of motivation, difficulty relaxing, difficulty sleeping, experiencing palpitations and dizziness, indigestion, diarrhoea or constipation, headaches, neck aches, backache, extreme tiredness and drinking or smoking more than usual, if one does them at all.

But what is this thing called stress and how did it get to be so bad for us? Stress is the word commonly used for being under pressure and that is not necessarily a bad thing. We all know people who thrive on being under pressure. I have one friend who has taken a taxi to the airport to set off for a family holiday and has to ask it to park up en route while he rushes into a shop to do his holiday clothes shopping. The same friend spent the morning of his wedding day constructing a 'top' table long enough for the bride, groom and relatives in the wine bar which had been booked for the reception. It is how he functions.

When we talk of stress being bad for health, however, we tend to mean being under more pressure in life than we can comfortably tolerate. Caring companies are very concerned about occupational stress, which, the research tells us, can be caused by a variety of circumstances. These include: having too much responsibility; having too little responsibility; having responsibility but not authority; experiencing too much change too quickly; lack of firm direction from managers; incompetent colleagues; poor relationships with colleagues and bosses; poor communication in the workplace; lack of consultation; poor prospects; threat of redundancy; too much noise; too many interruptions; poor working environment; malfunctioning equipment; sexual harassment; and dealing with hostile members of the public. Yes, that should about cover it.

Many organisations have introduced or are introducing stress management programmes which tend to centre on interventions such as relaxation training, yoga and massage, meditation, autogenic training and self hypnosis and even counselling and psychotherapy on an individual basis, often to deal with stressful issues unrelated to the workplace.

But increasingly, this vision of stress the monster and the steps that must be taken to defeat it is coming into question. A very recent report called "Killing the messenger: the pathologising of the stress response"[9] has been generating interest from companies worldwide, keen to learn new more positive strategies for tackling what has been termed stress.

The report was commissioned by the University of East Anglia's Centre for Environmental and Risk Management (CERM) which is an interdisciplinary centre providing a research and consultancy service to Government, industry and the public sector. It also acts as a World Health Organisation collaborating centre on environmental health risk assessment and communication. To produce the report, researchers "collated and analysed research data on 'stress' and 'occupational stress' across an interdisciplinary spectrum. It found that urgent reappraisal is needed, both of the 'stress as a disease' concept and of the current 'stress management' policy and practice". As a result of the worldwide interest the report has encouraged, an organisation called Strex Ltd has been established to act as a consultancy for companies wanting to put in place new strategies in the light of the findings from new research detailed in the report.

All this is very germane to what I am talking about in this book, so I shall look at their findings in some depth.

The role of stress

The reaction of stress is an instinctive and ancient survival mechanism, triggered by dangerous or novel stimuli which might require us to make a quick response. In olden times, this might take the form of meeting a wild boar. The stress response (all that goes along with the experience of fear) would gear us to take appropriate action, typically 'fight or flight'. I shall have more to say about 'fight or flight' in chapter 5 but suffice to say here that the stress response is an alarm system, calling our attention to possible threat. Yet since around the beginning of the 1980s a whole industry seems to have developed around stress, in which the physiological changes associated with stress have gradually become seen as the problem, the threat itself. As the report compellingly describes it: "Stress arousal is associated with accessing of inner resources

... It has high survival value. But the stress response functions as an alarm system. It is not meant to be ignored, any more than a burglar alarm is meant to be ignored. In the UK in the 1980s and 90s, however, a strange thing has happened. The burglar alarm is under 'new management'. It is no longer seen as a vital ally, a mechanism to galvanise the owner into mental or physical activity, enhance awareness and prompt adaptation to change and challenge. Instead, it is itself perceived as a dangerous menace, to be quietened down, switched off, or removed from the wall altogether".

The man usually credited with starting off all the interest in stress was endocrinologist Hans Selye, who first wrote about it in 1936. It was he, however, who also appears to deserve the discredit for causing the confusion which seems to have reigned ever since, as sometimes he referred to stress as the stimulus of physiological changes and other times as the response. The authors of the current report believe that the word stress is utterly unscientific and should be abandoned.

They also make numerous recommendations, all focusing on the need for stress symptoms to be recognised for what they are – an alert to the fact that something in one's environment needs dealing with, changing or adapting to – and not something to be dampened down and soothed away, whether with massage, relaxation, drugs, drink or binge eating. The latter are avoidance strategies and are a less effective response to whatever is causing stress than problem solving and solution focused strategies.

Among their recommendations they advise that individuals should cease to fear the physiological changes associated with the stress response (eg panic, pounding heart), thinking they herald disease, but act on them. (It is un-acted on stress signals that lead to illnesses.) They warn against resorting to excessive physical exercise as a way of dealing with stress, as research shows that stressing the body is actually more damaging than stressing the mind. In fact they recommend moderate stressing of the mind, as a means of using the mind to figure out ways to take more control over one's life, to make effective decisions, prioritise, etc, etc. They firmly warn against succumbing to learned helplessness, in the form of 'resignation, martyrdom and helplessness in dealing with problems' and promote facing up to challenges and threats, seeking specialist help in doing so, if necessary. All sources of stress need to be identified and addressed, individually. Obviously an individual can't do it all, if work culture prevents, but there are many steps that *can* be taken

For companies, they firmly recommend finding methods of raising morale, creating open channels of communication and constructive ways of resolving conflicts. It is to be hoped that all the interest shown in the report by so many companies will in due course be acted upon in a way that has positive benefits for all.

Thinking the best of oneself

Maslow set the need for esteem (from oneself for oneself and from others) high up in his hierarchy, positioning it as one of the unique human needs.

Rosenberg thought of self esteem as expressing an attitude towards oneself of either approval or disapproval[10] and believed it had three components: reflected appraisal, which is how we think that others see us; social comparison, where we compare ourselves with others; and self attribution, which describes the process of coming to conclusions about ourselves based upon how successful we think our efforts and actions are.[11] Others have shown that strong self esteem is an important element in positive handling of negative circumstances which might otherwise set off the stress alarms. The higher the self esteem, the lower also the risk of depression.

The importance of self esteem for effective functioning in the workplace has recently been demonstrated by clinical psychologists at the Institute of Psychiatry in London, and a consultant psychiatrist and a mental health nursing sister from Forest Healthcare Trust.[12] Called the Claybury CPN Stress Study, it was a survey of stress, coping and burnout in mental health nurses in what was at the time known as the North East Thames Region. They involved community mental health nurses from 15 of its 16 districts and ward based nurses in five large mental hospitals and two district hospital psychiatric units.

The nurses filled in a number of questionnaires, including Rosenberg's modified self esteem scale, to establish levels of self esteem, general health, coping skills and degree of burnout. From these it emerged, not surprisingly, that people who described themselves as more happy in their lives and those who considered they had job security generally had higher self esteem. Marital status, sex and qualifications had no bearing on self esteem but, importantly for our purposes, a supportive relationship with the line manager was very much associated with higher self esteem. Those who drank and smoked the most had correspondingly lower self esteem. The higher the nurses' self esteem, the higher their coping skills and sense of personal accomplishment and the lower their exhaustion levels. There was also half the sickness absence among those with high self esteem.

The researchers concluded that levels of stress, burnout and use of coping skills appeared to be closely related to degree of self esteem. They say that further exploration needs to be carried out to find out the factors that relate to the development of self esteem, how it is maintained and how it is eroded. Could self esteem enhancement courses be useful, they wonder. However, common sense can point us quite a lot of the way, here, and it points back to all the kinds of things we have been discussing so far. The more an individual feels valued – from their own view of themselves, from what they see is valued in others and from how they and others value what they do – the higher their self esteem is likely to be, the greater their job satisfaction and the lower the likelihood of their being exposed to more than unavoidable risks to their safety.

Take a risk

The attraction of adventure sports such as bungee jumping, parachuting, hang-gliding, abseiling, etc, has increased over the last few years. Many people, it seems, like to take risks. Taking risks is part of human nature. This stems from primitive times when even finding food or a safe place to live was a risk. In modern society our basic needs are taken care of and possibly this is why we feel the need to challenge ourselves and take risks in other ways.

Even today we *need* to take risks, reasonable risks. It can actually be good for our coping skills. Martin Zuckerman carried out a lot of research in the 1970s on people he called sensation seekers (they enjoyed activities which were exciting and scary), monitoring electrical activity in their brains when exposed to stressful stimuli. His findings led him to suggest that high sensation seeking confers a degree of protection because it enables people to raise their threshold for tolerating arousal and thus to cope better with negative life circumstances. [13] These are the sort of people who more often view problems as challenges. Whereas those who are low sensation seekers and don't like thrills and spills, perhaps even fear them, may be less likely to cope well with negatively arousing situations.

We need a degree of arousal to function well. We feel the blood pumping before making a presentation, before going on stage, before taking an exam, before running the race – and it gets us going, gets us ready to give our best. But too much can be incapacitating, if we cannot cope with it.

In many current work situations, however, we are largely denied the chance to take risks. When conformity is the aim, the corporate mission statement produces staff who are told what to do, when to do it and how to dress. It is supposed to ensure the reliability of the end product. In fact it anaesthetises. Production lines and systematic management take away any degree of creativity or initiative from the individual on the 'shop floor'. Yet in retail and in hospitals and in other service industries it is these people, not the management, who are in the frontline. It is these people who see the customer or patient first – not the higher paid manager in the back office or the much higher paid executive making policy back at head office. Yet, if frontline staff are not encouraged to deal with problems creatively and use their own initiative – stepping in to avert disasters which could culminate in violence by what I would term constructive risk taking (more of that in a later chapter) – it will be impossible for employers to deliver the customer care and satisfaction that enables them to meet targets or stay ahead of the opposition.

The negative side of the nannying mentality is that unreasonable risks often end up being taken. I should like to propose my hierarchy of risk, in the style of Maslow's hierarchy. As level is added on level, so risk of violence and injury rises. I start with lack of management leadership and understanding and a corresponding lack of motivation in the individual to do their job well. This sets the background scene for out of control emotions. Add to that lack of self worth, low self esteem and low self confidence and we are concocting a dangerous brew. The climate is one of resentment and fear, not one where individuals will be able to call on reserves of effective coping skills. Next add ego needs. If there is a workforce who undertakes mundane and repetitive tasks as a large part of their job description or who feels unsupported and isolated by management, it is human nature for them to want an opportunity to re-establish their ego in an attempt to feel better about themselves. In the event of a confrontation with an angry member of the public, we don't want to look foolish or ineffectual and the less we think of ourselves – and think that others think of us – the more likely we are to plunge in without thinking, in order to save face. Our own feelings of hostility (towards management) which are seething beneath the surface are also ready to rise and encourage us to have a pop, in a situation where we think we can justify our aggression. More likely it just bursts out, not under control at all. If there is a customer or organisational problem, all it takes is a moment of overreaction for someone to get seriously hurt or killed.

Security cameras, panic buttons, agreed procedures and back up – all these are the more obvious means of adding to security for staff in the front line. But the chance to take reasonable risks, to handle stressful events with initiative and creativity, to develop and maintain self esteem and to feel motivated to do one's job well, these too are absolutely crucial elements in the provision of a safe environment for staff to work in.

1   Maslow, A (1954). *Motivation and Personality*. Harper and Row, New York.

2   Winterbottom, M (1953). The sources of achievement motivation in mothers' attitudes towards independence training. In D McClelland et al (eds) *The Achievement Motive*. Appleton-Century-Crofts, New York.

3   Rosen, B C and d'Andrade, R (1959). The psychosocial origins of achievement motivation. *Sociometry*, 22, 185-218.

4   Too clever by half. *The Therapist* (1998), 5, 4, 2.

5   Rosenthal, R and Jacobson L (1968). *Pygmalien in the Classroom: Teacher Expectations and Pupil Intellectual Development.* Holt, Rinehart and Winston, New York.

6   Seligman, M E P and Maier, S F (1967). Failure to escape traumatic shock. *Journal of Experimental Psychology,* 74, 1-9.

7   de Vellis, R F (1978). Cited in de Vellis, R F and Callahan, L F (1993) A brief measure of helplessness in rheumatic disease. *Journal of Rheumatology,* 20, 866.

8   Seligman, M E P (1975) *Helplessness: on depression, development and death.* Freeman, San Francisco.

9   *Killing the messenger: the pathologising of the stress response* (1998). Strex Ltd, Gosfield, Essex.

10 Rosenberg, M (1965). *Society and Adolescent Self Image.* Princeton University Press, Princeton, New York.

11 Rosenberg, M, Schooler, C and Shoenbach, C (1989). Self esteem and adolescent problems: modelling reciprocal effects. *American Sociological Review,* 54, 1004-1018.

12 Carson, J, Fagin, L, Brown D, Leary,J and Bartlett, H (1997). Self esteem . *NT Research,* 2, 5, 361-369.

13 Zuckerman, M (1983). *Biological Bases of Sensation Seeking, Impulsiveness and Anxiety.* Erlbaum, Hillsdale, New Jersey.

4 – REQUIREMENTS OF THE LAW

THIS CHAPTER is about the legal side of safety. But I must stress at the outset that ensuring staff safety should not be just a legality. It should be the moral obligation of every manager and director. When we ask people to deal with unreasonable situations and aggressive people we should at least give them the tools to do the job properly.

For those who deal with violence at work, whether attempting to arrest a criminal, control a violent prisoner, detain a shoplifter or deal with an aggressive and hostile patient, the risk of being assaulted or injuring another person is ever present. Quite how employees are expected to handle this may depend upon the specific nature of their work or the perceived risks they face.

A police officer or prison officer, for instance, should be trained in arrest and restraint, or control and restraint, techniques. Increasingly, however, many workers in other organisations are also routinely being trained in control and restraint procedures. However, if people are trained in such techniques but without a full understanding of what can aggravate explosive situations, they raise the risk of use of unreasonable force, and serious injury or death may on occasions occur. In one recent two-year period, 18 people died in police custody and since 1989 there have been at least seven deaths in prisons related to the use of physical force for restraint.

For most workers in more 'civilian' environments, such as retail, healthcare, public transport, education and any other public or corporate service that deals directly with the public, training in how to deal with aggressive people is at best sporadic and very often badly structured, leaving staff feeling anxious and unsupported, with only lip service having been paid to their safety needs. A strategic organisational problem can even arise, where a corporation's policy on dealing with aggressive and potentially violent situations is clear, yet guidance and training in how to put that policy into practice are not. This can result in employee belief that although the corporation is saying one thing, it actually means another. For instance, in certain companies, although a policy statement exists, employees and even some managers believe that what it says is not what their superiors really expect of them and therefore choose to continue putting themselves and other staff at risk by attempting to do things (restrain violent people, retrieve stolen goods) they have not been trained to do.

In some environments, dealing with such situations is sometimes even left to the discretion of the most senior member of staff present or the manager on duty. This can cause anxiety and fear and lead to feelings of injustice, threat, confusion, frustration and humiliation which in turn can result in moral indignation. In some instances, employees may become even more aggressive than their assailants.

These are some of the reasons why so many injuries occur. Put together, it is no wonder that the risk of causing serious injury or death escalates when attempting to arrest, detain or restrain violent people.

The law on our side

Health and safety legislation has always made employers responsible for staff wellbeing but quite what the position becomes when a staff member is confronted by angry members of the public has been somewhat grey. For instance, the Health and Safety at Work Act 1974, section 2 (2) (c) states: "It is the employer's responsibility to provide such information, instruction, training and supervision to support their duty of care. It is the employer's responsibility to ensure that employees receive such information, instruction, training and supervision, as is necessary, to ensure the health, safety and welfare of staff". The responsibility is there but nothing is spelt out in detail.

Regulation 7 (Procedures for serious or imminent danger) of the Management of Health and Safety at Work Regulations 1992 states that, where dangers exist, the employer must have established suitable procedures to be followed and also have the people to implement them. Employees and others who are exposed to serious and imminent danger must be informed of the nature of the hazard and the protective steps that need to be taken. The procedures must also allow for anyone exposed to danger to stop work and reach a place of safety. Regulation 11 specifies that employers must provide safety training to employees when they are recruited, when their job or responsibility is changed, when new equipment or technology is introduced or whenever the system of work changes.

Clearly these regulations were written with hazardous procedures or substances more in mind than the hazards posed by raging members of the public. And they have probably been interpreted that way by employers and staff alike.

Now, however, loopholes are being closed and responsibilities are being spelled out more fully. Recent changes to relevant laws make it crystal clear that employers have a duty to protect their employees in all circumstances they may find themselves in, and regardless of levels of losses that the employer may incur.

Changes to the Reporting of Injuries, Diseases and Dangerous Occurrences Regulations (RIDDOR) 1995, issued by the Health and Safety Executive and which have been in effect since April 1996, create a new definition of the word 'accident' to include "an act of non-consensual physical violence done to a person at work". Employees must not only report any incidents of physical violence resulting in death or major injury but any that leave someone incapable of carrying out their normal work for three days or more.

This change has enormous implications for employers. They are now unequivocally responsible for dealing with violence by ensuring they comply with health and safety statutes in reducing risk of injury to staff through providing safe systems of work, safe operating procedures and adequate staff training, and that all cases of violence are reported in the same way as any other 'accident' at work.

Manslaughter

Under changes to current laws and new laws proposed in the Law Commission report,[1] published on March 5, 1996, any injuries or deaths resulting from violence could be viewed as 'management failure' and/or 'negligence' if no preventive or pro-active measures are taken to reduce the risk. This can and should result in more prosecutions of those responsible within the organisation for ensuring staff safety and failing to do so. Law changes may also make individual employees more responsible for any deaths arising from taking inadvisable risks. So it is vital for everyone to know exact procedures to follow in the event of a potentially dangerous incident involving a member of the public.

Even under existing legislation, one managing director was imprisoned after being prosecuted for 'gross negligence' due to the death of an employee. The current legal situation is that involuntary manslaughter convictions may be reached on the grounds of: gross negligence (where a death results not from a pure accident but from a person not taking enough care, or showing wanton disregard for others' safety); recklessness in carrying out a lawful act (where a death occurs because the person responsible took a conscious risk, or failed to consider an obvious risk); and dangerous and unlawful acts (where a death is connected with a crime such as robbery, in which serious harm was not intended but might have been thought by a reasonable person as likely to occur – an offence known as constructive man-slaughter).

In the case concerned, a 21-year-old employee at a haulage firm was asphyxiated after he was sprayed in the face by toxic paint. None of the employees had been provided with adequate personal protective equipment, such as face masks, and a safe system of work was not in place. The police investigating the incident believed that the negligence of the company was so gross that a charge of manslaughter was justified. The managing director of the haulage company was sentenced to 12 months imprisonment. He was also fined £1,500 for breaches of section 2 (1) of the Health and Safety at Work Act 1974. The company was fined £7,000 under the same section and a further £1,500 for the charge of manslaughter.

According to the managing director's solicitor, the conviction showed that the charge of manslaughter brought against an employer, where the individual's negligence is defined as gross, means that acts of omission (a careless error) rather than commission (a deliberate action, uncaring of the consequences) can lead to a conviction. Importantly, the charge could equally apply to an employee in a supervisory position.

The new Law Commission report, which is concerned with the criminal liability of those who kill when they do not intend to cause death or serious injury, pays special attention to corporate responsibility for manslaughter. In the Draft Bill the Commission has submitted to Parliament, offences of involuntary manslaughter are to be replaced with the new offence of reckless killing and killing by gross carelessness. The offence of corporate manslaughter is to be replaced by the new offence of corporate killing. This has major implications for both employees and employers.

Reckless killing means someone causing the death of another when aware of the risk that his conduct will cause death or serious injury or that it is unreasonable for him to take that risk, in the circumstances.

A person can be convicted of killing by gross carelessness if: a risk that his conduct will cause death or serious injury would be obvious to a reasonable person in his position; he is capable of appreciating the risk at the time; and either his conduct falls far below that which could reasonably be expected of him in the circumstances or else he intends to cause some injury or is aware of, or unreasonably takes, the risk that it may do so. This puts considerably more onus on the individual to think about the consequences of his actions and act accordingly.

The law on corporate manslaughter is to be changed because a successful prosecution currently requires one specific person to be identified as the "controlling mind" of the company. As a result there have been only four prosecutions for corporate manslaughter under English law and only one conviction, after the 1993 Lyme Bay canoeing disaster in which four people died.

Because that case concerned a one-man company, there was no difficulty in identifying a controlling mind responsible. In other cases, the requirement has turned out to be insuperable.

The new offence of corporate killing proposed by the Commission would make a corporation liable to prosecution where its conduct falls far below that which could reasonably be expected of the corporation in the circumstances and where such conduct results in a death. This unacceptably dangerous conduct is termed "management failure" in the report and concerns the employer's duty to ensure a safe system of work. The Commission suggests that there is no reason not to extend this term to include a failure to provide safe premises or equipment or competent staff. This offence could be deemed to occur even if the risk is not obvious or the defendant is incapable of appreciating it. Management failure need not be the immediate cause of death.

In the report, the Zeebrugge ferry disaster was cited as an illustration of where the new offence might apply. The prosecution against P&O European Ferries failed after the judge directed the jury to acquit the company and the five most senior individual defendants. The main reason for his decision was that there was insufficient evidence to convict any one individual defendant on the facts and that, without one such individual, the company could not be convicted of corporate manslaughter.

In any such circumstances in the future, under the new offence the failure of a company to devise a safe system for the operation of its ferries could be a management failure which fell far below that which could reasonably have been expected, enabling a conviction for corporate killing.

> (The Law Commission report defines a company as guilty of corporate killing if:
>
> 1   a management failure by the corporation is the cause or one of the causes of a person's death; and either
>
> 1.1   there is a management failure by a corporation if the way in which its activities are managed or organised fails to ensure the health and safety of persons employed in or affected by those activities; and
>
> 1.2   such a failure may be regarded as a cause of a person's death notwithstanding that the immediate cause is the act of omission of an individual.
>
> 2   That failure constitutes conduct falling far below what can reasonably be expected of the corporation in the circumstances.)

The new offence, if adopted, is intended to extend to all corporations, irrespective of the legal means by which they are incorporated. So not only those incorporated under a general public Act (such as the Companies Act 1985) but also by common law, royal charter, etc, would be covered.

Only a corporation could face a charge of corporate killing. Directors and managers would not face prosecution for the offence. But if the particular acts or omissions of particular individuals were a contributing cause to death, director might be prosecuted under the Commission's suggested replacement for involuntary manslaughter: reckless killing or killing by gross carelessness.

The Home Office is currently considering the Law Commission's report. It is for Ministers to decide whether to put forward legislation to enact the Commission's recommendations, but the Labour Party has backed introducing the new offence at the first opportunity. This new law would sit very comfortably with current health and safety at work legislation to enforce accountability on those who are responsible for the safety of others.

There are other law changes in the pipeline which will also add weight to the responsibilities of employers for safety, and muscle to others for enforcing them. At some time in the next 18 months there will be a Human Rights Act to replace the European Convention's Bill of Human Rights. This will provide courts with a pro-active means of dealing with dangerous situations, instead of, as at present, only having reactive means available. Judges will be enabled to rely on their own discretion when making decisions, instead of being dependent on case law. Also offering some new possibilities is the new Crime and Disorder Act.

The Crime and Disorder Act

This Act became law in July 1998. In a speech to the Magistrates' Association in Blackburn the month before,

Home Secretary Jack Straw described it like this: "The Crime and Disorder Bill {as it then was} has a simple ambition: to help build a safer and more responsible society. It is a big Bill, running to some 119 clauses and 10 schedules... In this great bulk, the Bill has three key themes:

- first, reforming youth justice to focus efforts on *preventing* offending by children and young people;

- second, building safer communities, through new local partnerships and by giving better protection against antisocial behaviour, sex offenders and drug misusing offenders;

- third, criminal justice reform to improve performance, reduce delays and promote public confidence in the system".

My friend John Gridley, crime prevention design adviser for the Metropolitan Police, has had 21 years' experience of crime prevention work, including community safety which forms a major part of the Act. I asked him to explain how he sees it working for the benefit of ordinary people who may be at risk while doing their daily jobs.

"The Crime and Disorder Act," he said, "is about people working in partnership to prevent crime and disorder in the interests of community safety. Traditionally different groups have worked independently but the Act makes it mandatory that people work together. This means the police and the local authorities and contributory agencies, such as health authorities, education, probation and youth services. Other partners are the 'community' including, for instance, residents' associations and neighbourhood watch groups, and the private sector, such as local shops and other businesses.

"Each local authority has to do an audit of crime and disorder in their area, define what needs to be done to reduce the problems – say, burglary, criminal damage, assaults – and have a community safety strategy written and in place by April 1999. The strategy must also cover how they plan to get the message out to all who need to know it. For instance, this might be through meetings with community groups, minority groups, public meetings, advertisements in local newspapers and so on. Every three years the whole process has to be repeated, starting with new audits of crime.

"So what might it mean in practice? Suppose someone hasn't paid their gas bill and a gas fitter is given the address and told to cut off the gas supply there, not knowing that there might be a violent confrontation awaiting him. At present he might simply arrive, knock on the door and say that he has come to cut the household off. That shouldn't happen. He shouldn't have to knock on a door where he knows the occupants won't be at all pleased to see him and not know whether there is an old lady, an old lady with a strapping son, or a family with a history of violent assault on the other side.

"Under the new Act, the gas company would contact the police and local authority – it's early days yet but perhaps there might be a community safety committee, involving police, health, probation, local authorities etc, and the administrator of the gas company can just contact the administrator of the committee – and ask whether there is any known risk to the fitter if he goes to that house. The relevant partners can carry out searches – for instance, for a criminal record for violent assault or for a history of mental illness and violence. The housing department's check might reveal that the occupants are a problem family who have been rehoused several times and the wife has repeatedly been battered by the husband, although there has never been charges and he has no record. The company now knows what the fitter might be up against and what precautions to take, to comply with the Health and Safety at Work Act.

"By working in partnership and sharing information beforehand, it should be possible to avert some otherwise inevitable disasters. It means, for instance, that a district nurse going to a new patient to dress a leg ulcer shouldn't have to assume when she knocks on the door that all is okay on the other side. She should be able to expect that a number of agencies will have done their homework and found out whether the patient has a history of violence. If the patient does have a history of assault, she should expect to make the visit accompanied by a colleague. She should expect that whatever support services she needs are either there, if appropriate, or will be available to help her, if needs be, and she should expect to be able to summon them instantly by alarm or radio.

"Suppose a woman feels nervous at night walking down the unlit alley that leads to her local station. She can make this known at a public meeting or by contacting the community safety team. Someone would then investigate and find, perhaps, that the railway owns that land, so they need to be told to take the steps to make it safer. Also, there appear to be overhanging branches from adjoining gardens which are adding to the general gloom and creepiness. The owners can be alerted to cut these back. All this, of course, could have been done without the Crime and Disorder Act. But such rights are rarely enforced. What the Act does is prepare the ground so that systems are in place and every agency knows the part they should play. And it *will* be enforced.

"Having so many different agencies involved, with the common aim of making life safer for individuals, also means fresh approaches can be taken to thorny old problems. For instance, in a run down area, a group of youths regularly used to enter a particular store, committing theft and criminal damage. When they were chased by shop staff the youths would run out of the shop and across the road where they would arm themselves with stones and bricks from a pile of rubble.

They then pelted the pursuing store staff with them. The police contacted the local authority and the local authority instructed the highways department to clean away the rubble. Other local authority departments assisted in the swift removal of graffiti from the surrounding site – if graffiti is allowed to stay, more joins it and the more run down an area becomes – and in improving the street lighting. Once the 'ammunition' was gone and the area was cleared, cleaned and lit, the whole problem ceased.

"In any workplace, we all know the reception area is the most vulnerable. So the design of reception areas is crucial; they must always be welcome areas designed to reduced aggression. In places where violence might be expected, such as accident and emergency departments, there should be no 'ammunition' like loose chairs or vending machines that aren't fixed to the floor or wall. The security staff area should be next to reception, not way off in a little hut at the back somewhere. The reception desk should be nice and wide, so angry customers can't lean across it. 'Barriers' of some kind should stop anyone being able to wander past reception when receptionists are busy. And so on and so forth. With partnership, one can get together everyone who matters – the owners of the building, the architects, the planners, the workers – and design safety into the layout."

John Gridley has cared about crime prevention for a very long time and clearly has high hopes of this Act. As he succinctly puts it: "By getting partners together, a lot of crime can be designed out altogether."

Who pays?

Companies who don't take their responsibilities for providing a safe working environment seriously could well suffer in other ways besides through the courts. For example employers' liability insurance cover, designed to protect a corporation against statutory liability for injury to employees arising out of their employment, may not pay out if it is found that a safe workplace or safe system of work does not exist. In the case of tackling aggressive or violent people, this means ensuring a safe procedure is in place and known about, so that every employee who might possibly encounter such a danger is aware of what they are expected to do – and, just as importantly, what they are *not* expected to do.

Public liability cover, on the other hand, protects the corporation and its employees against liability arising out of all trading activities. So if a person is injured by a member of staff, the corporation is protected and any action would be defended by the insurers. However, in certain circumstances, the individual employee might be sued. That employee would only be covered by the corporation insurance if *he/she did not act outside the requirements of his/her employment.* In other words, if an employee uses excessive force (and I shall be coming on to talking about that shortly), they may not be covered and may even have to face criminal charges brought by the police.

The need for training

I think we have seen quite clearly now that employers are supposed to train staff to deal with any dangerous circumstances that arise. They have a legal duty to do so. That doesn't mean they must arrange for all staff to take self defence classes or learn control and restraint techniques. What they must do is offer clear guidance and training in how to handle the situation without themselves or the assailant getting hurt. *That requirement applies as much to an employer of one (a boss and secretary, a single-handed GP and his receptionist) as it does to employers of large numbers.*

Progress, however, has been rather slow in this direction. While some organisations really haven't taken the requirements on board, others are trying really hard. The October 28 1998 issue of the *Nursing Times*, which introduced its Stamp Out Violence Campaign, highlighted what a number of trusts were starting to put in place. Responses included more two-way radios, closed circuit TVs and control-locked doors. Others disliked the idea of too much locking and unlocking, especially in the need to respond to medical emergencies, and were opting for more uniformed security presence. Some have set up violence hotlines. Some are teaching staff self defence, control and restraint and breakaway techniques. Others are trying to teach staff how to defuse situations safely.

It would seem as though there is no consensus as to what works best. Everyone is taking a shot in the dark. And in some settings, the situation is deteriorating instead of improving. Early this year, *The Independent* newspaper published details[2] of Prison Service security reports which it had seen and which showed that fewer than 40 per cent of prison officers and only 10 per cent of prison governors were legally competent to carry out control and restraint procedures, even though all prison staff are supposed to be taught them. At Wakefield prison, only 17 per cent of prison officers were trained in restraining prisoners.

This ludicrous and dangerous situation has arisen because of an attempt to *increase* safety. To avoid injury to inmates through inept handling, prison officers may now only carry out control and restraint measures if they have undergone at least eight hours refresher training in the previous 12 months. It is not happening. This means that, in the event of violence or even a riot, most prison staff should not touch an inmate in an attempt to restrain them.

This is a classic situation where staff know the regulations but perceive employers as expecting something else from them – assistance, however ham-fisted, in the event of colleagues or other inmates being put at risk. However, if a restraint situation is handled by a team where one or more members is less competent than required, it can quickly escalate out of all control.

Once control is lost, the risk of injury or death increases dramatically. So, if staff are not competently trained, they not only have a right to withdraw from a dangerous situation, they have a duty to do so. (The Prison Service, when contacted by *The Independent*, said it was seeking to rectify any deficiencies in refresher training as soon as possible.)

What is reasonable force?

Knowing the answer to the above question is important because it may make all the difference not only in a court of law, but also when implementing company policy and\or strategy, and when dealing with staff development issues such as staff training. In a confrontational situation, priority must be given to the safety of all involved, and this includes the person who is causing all the trouble.

We know we may be entitled to use force in our own self defence or that of others, but, even here, what is justified and what is not? The law of self defence, as applied by the courts, specifies two basic requirements: the force used must have been both necessary and reasonable. A way of measuring whether this was so is to apply "the proportionality standard". That means trying to define whether the amount of force used was in 'balance' or 'in proportion to' the crime being committed. This is not to say that if someone is threatened with immediate unexpected assault they are to weigh up the 'niceties of law' before defending themselves. But it certainly should be considered when, for example, attempts are being made to catch a fleeing thief, especially if the only reason we have encountered the thief is because we are employed as a retail store manager or shop assistant. In this case it would be totally unreasonable and unnecessary to use the degree of force which we might have a right to use if we ourselves were under serious attack.

Put another way, force of an extreme and dangerous nature (which may result in the death of another) could be deemed justified if used in the preservation of our own or another's life. But the same use of force would not be deemed justified if it were used, say, to 'teach someone a lesson' in circumstances where risk of loss of life is not the issue – for example, detaining a shop thief or hitting out at someone who has sworn at you.

The interpretation of whether force is justified or not also depends upon the circumstances. In establishing the facts of a case a court must interpret the issues of justification and proportionality. Pertinent factors in this process include:

- the gravity of the crime being prevented;
- whether it was possible to prevent the crime by non-violent means;
- whether you were ready to try those means first;
- the relative strength of the parties involved.

Use of physical force resulting in injury or death is not justified in cases such as attempted shoplifting, for instance, especially if prior knowledge that the act of theft is taking place could have enabled the situation to have been handled in a more controlled manner. One American shoplifter managed to get compensation for damage done to his shoulder in the course of a struggle to deprive him of his stolen goods. Very commonly there are other means that can be tried first, as we shall see in the final two chapters. Not trying those means because 'having a go' actually provides an outlet for any pent up angry feelings of our own (eg about being taken for granted or not being respected at work) also deprives us of justification for saying our use of force was reasonable. As for the relative strength of the parties involved, well, that is not straightforward at all.

Relative strength

Let's imagine that I want to restrain an aggressive patient who is threatening me and other members of staff. Let's also imagine that the strength of the patient is represented by 10 units and mine is represented by eight units. In other words, he is stronger than me. However, I have four colleagues with me whose strength on average is represented as eight units each. We now have 40 units of strength, which makes us four times stronger than our aggressive patient, and, in theory, we need use only a third of our collective strength to overpower him. However, without proper training, we are each more likely to be aware only that the patient is stronger than we are, individually. So we work independently and apply all of our five times eight units of force against his 10. It is in such circumstances that the person we were only trying to restrain may easily be injured and killed - and we will not be deemed to have used reasonable force.

It takes only about eight and a half pounds of applied pressure to break any bone in the human body – and less than two pounds of applied pressure to kill. On to all that we have to add the effects of our emotions. Fear, panic and determination to save someone else's life can increase physical strength – in the way that a mother might sometimes be able to lift the front of a car, if her child is trapped beneath it. Only recently I was running a training seminar where I was explaining that, and one of the delegates responded that he had had a similar experience. He had been in the street when a Volvo car crashed and turned over. Desperate to help the occupants get out, he wrenched at the door and it came off completely in his hands. He was surprised but assumed the door must have been damaged or weakened by the impact, and his main concern was that the passengers all made it to safety. However, when the firefighters arrived, they told him that the Volvo door was not damaged. In his panic to help, he had not realised his own strength. Afterwards, he said, it made him shake to realise just how strong he could, if necessary, be.

Anger is another emotion that increases strength. If we have strong negative feelings about our attacker and if we are also fearful, which is highly likely, the degree of force we actually apply is likely to escalate.

The causes of serious injury

Serious injury or death is generally caused when the functioning of the respiratory, circulatory or nervous systems is damaged or interfered with. This can happen in a number of ways, as a result of trying to control and restrain another person for their own safety or that or others.

One not uncommon scenario occurs because of heightened resistance to pain triggered by the release of endorphins, chemicals which block the transmission of pain signals when the body is under extreme stress. Someone who is out of control and whom others are trying to restrain may struggle for longer and more strongly because of abnormal pain tolerance. However, with stress levels escalating all the time, he may suddenly reach a state of extreme exhaustion, enabling restraint measures finally to be successful, and then collapse almost completely. If he is, at that point, in the restraint position, face down on the floor with arms immobilised behind his back or perhaps with the weight of other people on him, he may not even have the strength to breathe. So death can then occur frighteningly quickly, without those trying to restrain him for his own safety even realising for crucial moments the tragic consequences of their well intentioned actions.

It is essential during and more especially after a restraint for those doing the restraining to make sure the person under control has a clear airway, that chest movement is not impeded (eg by hands being restrained behind the back) and to observe respiratory rate. It is also wise to check how many people are still applying pressure to the person's back, neck and shoulders, as it is unchecked weight and force that can accelerate a state of asphyxia.

Sometimes untrained people almost instinctively try to restrain a violent person by grabbing them around the neck to restrain them or try to bring them to the ground. However, when a person is in a heightened state of physiological arousal (to be explained fully in the next chapter), pressure in the region of the carotid sinus (below the angle of the jaw) can lead to sudden slowing or even stoppage of the heart, an effect more likely to occur and to be fatal if associated with exertion.

People already suffering from coronary heart disease, hypertension or diabetes are at increased risk of cardiac arrest if they have been struggling or deprived of oxygen. Struggle and anxiety plus other emotions increase the risk of a potentially fatal asthma attack in an asthma sufferer. Sufferers of sickle cell disorders (which are inherited conditions and quite common in black African populations) are also at raised risk as blockages to the circulatory system can quickly occur under conditions of low oxygen, such as extreme physical exertion and arousal. This in turn can cause a heart attack or stroke which could be fatal.

Certain mental disorders can also cause excitation and aggression in the sufferer. People suffering from psychosis may become extremely disoriented and confused and may believe others are intent on causing them harm. If they become frightened and agitated, they may become aggressive and violent.

Another state in which people may believe their personal safety is under threat is known as excited delirium. It can be caused by psychiatric illness or by drug intoxication or both. (Cocaine is the best known cause of drug-induced psychosis.) Many will have negative or uncertain expectations of those who represent authority and may also feel that way about anyone trying to help them.

Both these individuals and those suffering from psychosis will have an increased level of strength matched by an increased tolerance to pain, matched again by their tendency to experience fatigue very suddenly after a violent struggle.

We are unlikely to know the medical history of someone who is being violent and may appear to need to be restrained. And most people don't know the possible adverse consequences of restraint methods used without the utmost care. All we do know is that what seemed at the time to have been reasonable force may turn out not to be so reasonable after all. In 1995 a 21-year-old girl named Zoe Fairley, who had learning difficulties, died during restraint when four care workers held her face down on the floor. Fourteen-stone Zoe had flown into a tantrum at the social services hostel where she sometimes stayed, kicking over a coffee table and running at the group leader, punching the air. The group leader and another carer managed to force her to the ground but said they had to call for more help as they were losing control. She was restrained by two carers putting pressure on a shoulder each, one putting pressure on her legs and another pressing down on her buttocks. The restraint went on for 30 minutes.

The group leader was reported as saying: "After some time Zoe seemed to have calmed down so we gradually got off her one by one. She did not move – which was not uncommon – but we soon realised something was wrong when her left hand looked blue and her arm was limp".

Zoe was in effect crushed to death and died from asphyxia "due to compression of the trunk", according to a Home Office pathologist. The emergency services were called but could not revive her.

So, to sum up, our aim must be to find a balance between doing what is justifiably necessary while suppressing the urge for retaliation and retribution. As Dicey, professor of law at Oxford University in the 1900s, explained it; "the right of self help must, from the nature of things, be a compromise between the necessity, on the one hand, of allowing every citizen to maintain his rights against wrongdoers, and the necessity, on the other hand, of suppressing private warfare..."[3] If there is a risk of foreseeable violence which arises from the nature of our employment, employers *must* take whatever steps, so far as is practicable and necessary to minimise the risk to staff.

Breakaway techniques

Many companies and organisations have for a number of years incorporated training in 'breakaway techniques' into their measures for ensuring the personal safety of their staff. Breakaway techniques are meant to provide a non-violent means of defending oneself against an attacker. They are supposed to enable someone to remove themselves from the grasp of another person without causing any injury to the attacker. These techniques are meant to bridge the gap between control and restraint training (which uses physical force to restrain another person for their own or someone else's protection) and self defence (designed purely for the protection of oneself).

However breakaway techniques are limited in their application and are therefore potentially dangerous. In one training video I have seen, various different techniques applicable for various different threat situations are shown. To simplify the issues, the areas of threat are grouped as attacks against the head, torso and arms, and then a number of techniques are demonstrated which could be used to deal with attacks to these three predominant areas. The video also shows how these breakaway techniques can be 'put together' to enable the individual to break away from a situation comprising a number of different attacks.

But it is simply not good practice to teach a person a wide range of techniques designed for a wide range of attacks – they will forget more than they remember! It is also not good practice to teach a technique that entails a combination of two or three movements. However easily the movements may flow in the comfort and controlled environment of the training room, it is highly unlikely that they will be executed correctly in a stressful real life threat situation. Once again we could end up with a situation in which someone gets seriously hurt.

Imagine a nurse facing an angry patient holding a knife. Many nursing staff have undergone various physical skills training programmes such as control and restraint training and breakaway technique training to deal with enraged individuals, and on some courses they will have been shown defences against a knife attack as part of the syllabus. This may in itself be enough to make her to believe that she should try to take the patient on. Imbued with the belief that she needs to protect others, she thinks it is a 'requirement'. I have studied martial arts for about 25 years, and I have had the pleasure and the privilege of working with, and being trained by, some of the best in the industry. Knife defences work extremely effectively – *on the mat!* In a controlled environment, the trauma is not experienced. In reality, attempting to disarm or control a knife wielding aggressor with empty hand skills alone in a pressured and extremely stressful situation will only increase the opportunity for things to go very wrong indeed – especially if we believe we have a duty of care to the aggressor and, therefore, cannot harm them.

A knife is a very deadly weapon. Statistically, it has been shown that 30 per cent of individuals stabbed will die from their wounds as opposed to 10 per cent of people who are shot, yet we treat the knife as a lesser weapon than a firearm. This is compounded by the ridiculous techniques taught as 'defences against a knife' taught on breakaway technique courses which are in many cases useless, negligent, and even downright criminal in their construction and application.

If you are being physically held and all the reasonable attempts you have made to remove yourself have failed, and you feel there is a real threat to your personal safety, you are within your rights to use physical force to remove yourself from the danger. But physical force must be used only as a last resort and as a means either to "preserve life" (survive the threat), or to create a "window of opportunity to escape", nothing more. Force used outside of these purposes could lead to charges ranging from common assault to murder.

However, if by the very nature of our employment we are exposed to risks that we would not otherwise normally encounter, it is the employer's duty to ensure that everything possible is done to reduce or eliminate such risks through physical security measures, safe working practices, and competent staff training. No employer should rely on the common law right of individuals to defend themselves. This is why police officers are equipped with batons, CS spray, handcuffs and firearms.

One of the big problems today, however, is that, while many organisations are at last starting to try and provide training for their staff so that they know methods for defusing violent situations without putting either themselves or their attackers at risk, they are going the wrong way about it. These methods focus on creating rapport and communicating with the potential assailant as they stand there ranting and raving before you, brandishing a weapon or punching and kicking out. But it is impossible to communicate and interact if you are terrified. The body just doesn't work that way. And that is what I want to explain in the next chapter.

1 *Legislating the Criminal Code: involuntary manslaughter* (1996). Law Commission No 237.

2 Prison staff lack training to restrain aggressive inmates. *The Independent,* Thursday February 12, 1998.

3 Dicey, A V (1885, eighth edition, 1915). The *Law of the Constitution* . Macmillan, London.

CHAPTER 5   PEOPLE UNDER THREAT

"I saw the man coming down the corridor towards me. Then I saw something glinting in his hand and realised it was a knife. I just froze."

"I turned the corner and saw two men standing at the far end of the street. It was just something in the way they stopped talking and looked at me. I turned round again and fled."

"I don't know what it was. I thought I was keeping calm. Then he said those words and something went flash inside me and I'd hit him before I knew it."

These are all responses to fear and threat. When we feel threatened by the behaviour of other people, we may act in any of a number of ways according to the circumstances, sometimes without even realising what we are doing. What I always teach people is that we can never control other people's behaviour. But we can learn to control our own responses. In a risky situation, we can learn to act in a way that makes us master of the options.

But to have a better chance of doing that, first we need to understand some of the basic biology that explains – and can help us defuse – aggression.

The evolution of the brain

I am going to start off by talking about the human brain. The brain of our ancestors was pretty small. It was about half a litre in volume – about the size of a modern chimpanzee's brain, and also about the size of the engine capacity of a Fiat 500. The human brain is about three times bigger, equivalent in size to the engine of a sports car. Most of what we know about the functioning of different parts of the brain has been known to us only over the last few decades and some of what we know is actually extremely recent indeed. In most textbooks that covered the brain, it was standard to quote that we only knew what 10 per cent of the brain was designed to do. Now, however, with new scanning techniques which enable scientists to look at the brains of living people while they are actually doing or feeling things that make the relevant parts of their brain light up, we are well on the way to understanding it all.

For our purposes, we need to know a little only about a few areas of the brain. The human brain is the size of a coconut. The largest and most highly developed part is called the cerebrum. It is composed of two hemispheres, covered with folded grey tissue known as the cerebral cortex. The cerebrum is responsible for initiating and coordinating all of the body's voluntary activities and it also governs the way the lower parts of the nervous system function. The cerebral cortex is where all intelligent behaviour takes place. It accounts for 40 per cent of the size of our brains and contains billions of neurons, the electrical impulses which carry information. The cerebral cortex is the part of the brain most directly responsible for what we term consciousness. It is heftily involved in the acts of perception, thinking, memory, planning and the understanding of emotion.

At the back of this area of brain, sticking out at the base and partly connected to it, lies the cerebellum (literally, the 'little brain'). When our far distant ancestors were alive, this part made up almost all of their brain. The reason that we are able to carry out new skills automatically lies in the cerebellum. It stores all the practice movements we learn, from riding a bike to playing a piano to driving a car. It creates movement or action without our needing to apply conscious thought to the task, so the higher part of the brain is free to pursue or be alert to other challenges. A thought triggers the process of making the movement, then the cerebellum takes over and we are operating on automatic. It took about two and a half million years for our cerebral cortex to evolve from the cerebellum of our ancestors.

Another part of the brain that is older still is the limbic system, which is also situated beneath the cerebrum. It is concerned with primitive urges, such as the need for food and sex and it is here that emotions are generated. It also feeds information upwards to the cortex. So, for instance, fear may be registered in the limbic system and relayed to the higher cortex which makes the conscious decisions about circumstances, consequences, possible implications, etc, which may influence how we decide to act. (Note, that is act, not react. The emotional response is automatic.) Fear is registered in an area called the amygdala.

The emotional manager

The amygdala is an almond shaped cluster of interconnected structures located at the bottom of the limbic system, near the edge of the brainstem (which is the oldest part of the brain. It developed about 500 million years ago and deals with unconscious processes such as breathing, heartbeat and blood pressure.).

Recent research by American emotion researcher Joseph LeDoux[1] has shown how the architecture of the brain gives the amygdala a privileged position as the brain's emotional manager. The amygdala, in effect, acts as a storehouse for emotional memory. And it is the amygdala which affects our behaviour in situations of heightened emotional stress. We think of emotions as any of quite a wide range of feelings but in fact emotions are very primitive and survival-oriented. They spur us to move away from danger or move towards something that satisfies a need. 'Higher' or more complex emotions, such as guilt, irritation or contempt, require a mental input from the higher cortex. The type of emotion the amygdala is concerned with is impulse.

So when impulsive feeling overrides rational thought,

the amygdala is at work. It operates like an early warning system of emotional arousal. When it receives incoming signals, it scans them for any signs of trouble. This places the amygdala in a pivotal position in our mental state. In essence, it is poised to perform in the way of something like an alarm company in our neural network.

For example, if we are confronted by a situation or person that causes us fear, the amygdala reacts instantly and spontaneously sends messages to all parts of the brain. The scenario is not dissimilar to our dialling 999 when we see a neighbour's house being broken into and being asked by the telephone operator which emergency service we require. It is the amygdala that dials 999. The response comes from the thinking part of the brain.

The amygdala is also sensitive to expressions. One part responds to facial expressions – a grimace, dilated pupils and reddened cheeks may signify anger – while another responds to tone. A trembling cry may signify fear in others and therefore possible threat to us too, a snarling voice may indicate anger and ill-intent.

The signals sent by the amygdala trigger our fear response – the ancient fight or flight response which I am going to describe more fully in a moment. When this happens, major changes take place in our behavioural and hormonal systems, gearing the body up to fight or run away. The amygdala acts as an 'action broker', mobilising the centres needed for movement and stimulating other necessary bodily functions. It even goes so far as to instruct the brainstem, the lowliest part of the brain, to fix the face in a fearful expression, the normal fear face of all primates. Movements unrelated to the immediate task at hand are frozen, while attention is riveted on the source of the fear and preparing the muscles to react in response to the perceived threat.

While all this is going on, cortical memories are shuffled and searched to retrieve any knowledge relevant to the emergency at hand, taking precedence and priority over any other strands of thought. This all occurs before any response is fully registered by the larger and higher part of the brain.

It used to be thought that the eyes, ears and other sensory organs routinely transmitted signals to a part of the brain called the thalamus and from there to the sensory processing areas of the higher brain, where the signals would come together to form objects as we perceive them. This is indeed what happens – but not when we are under stress or at risk from a perceived threat.

LeDoux discovered that there is a small bundle of neurons that leads directly from the thalamus to the amygdala, as well as neurons which take the larger pathway to the higher cortex. In his book *Emotional Intelligence*,[2] Daniel Goleman describes this shorter pathway as a "neural back alley", which allows the amygdala to receive some inputs directly from the senses and therefore start a response before they are fully registered in the higher brain centres of cerebral cortex. (LeDoux himself calls it "the quick and dirty route".)

What does this mean? It means that the amygdala does not depend upon the intelligent cerebral cortex for its stimulation but can act independently of it, creating its own emotional reactions. As the pathway to the amygdala is shorter, the amygdala can trigger the emotional response even as a parallel response is being considered in the higher cortex. In short, it can spring us into action while the slower, yet better informed, neocortex unfolds its more refined and detailed plan for action.

One drawback with this ability to react immediately to a situation of apparent threat is that the system is somewhat out of date. This is a system that was highly appropriate to a world where even finding food and a place to sleep was life threatening. It is appropriate to animals who instinctively know, for instance by smell, whether a newcomer is friend or foe. It is not always so useful when the possibilities are more diverse. So, if we hear a crashing noise outside a back window at night, we might have started to run out of the front door in panic into the driving rain and wind before we realise that in fact the commotion was probably caused by our hanging basket falling down. We may whirl round at the sound of an unexpected footstep and be ready to lash out in self protection, before realising that the newcomer is a family member whom we didn't know was in the house at the time.

It only takes a quarter of a second, however, before the higher brain receives the necessary information and quickly maps out a plan. If there is no threat, it will send a message down to say that there is no need for panic and everything can go back to where it was. If there really *is* a threat, the process the amygdala has started may be continued. But this may not always be appropriate either because, as already said, threatening situations that arise in modern day life are rarely so simple as in the wild. It isn't a case of let the bigger and better fighter win. It is a case of using intelligence to defuse what might otherwise become a dangerous situation to any or all involved in it. We have to learn to use our higher brain to bring the amygdala under control when, instinctively, we might in fact still be wanting to let it have its leash.

Unconscious memory and trauma

There is one final thing I want to say about the amygdala at this point. I said it was a storehouse for emotional memories. These are unconscious emotional memories. Conscious memories are stored in an area of the brain called the hippocampus and can be recalled at will. But we do not know we have stored unconscious memories nor, when they are triggered, are we likely to understand why we are experiencing the emotions associated with them. They are likely to explain, however, much of the experience of post traumatic stress.

In an article in *The Therapist*,[3] international trauma care expert Noreen Tehrani gave a compelling example of how this works. When someone undergoes a traumatic event, a 3D stereophonic depiction of the event is conveyed to the brain via the ears, eyes, skin, mouth and nose. In the case of one man whom she helped, who had been on a motorboat which capsized, he experienced, with graphic horror, the sensations of going under the water, seeing the colours of the water, feeling sudden coldness, swallowing water and smelling diesel fuel. The man recovered after the motorboat disaster and was able to resume his normal life. Yet, when he first went into a petrol station to fill up his car, he was filled with intense fear and experienced a panic attack. This happened again. Gradually he started to fear having panic attacks and began to experience them in other places too.

What happens in such cases is this. All the initial sensations associated with the traumatic experience (the cold, the wet, the smells, etc) pass to the thalamus where they are collected together and passed on to the amygdala. Here they are formed into a sensory memory which in turn is passed to the hippocampus and to the cortex and finally is translated into a verbal or narrative memory.

As we have already seen, part of the amygdala's job is to assess the emotional importance of whatever information is coming in and decide how strong an emotional response is required. The more life threatening the event, the stronger the response. If there is an overload of information to process, the sensory memories can't get through to the hippocampus and stay trapped in the amygdala as trauma memories instead of being translated and made sense of by the higher cortex. This trapped trauma memory has no identifiable meaning. It cannot be described, only experienced in the form of flashbacks, panic attacks and other forms of sensory re-experience.[4]

As Tehrani describes it: "Recall of information trapped

within the trauma memory of the amygdala is emotion state dependent.[5] Some pieces of sensory information associated with the event require a certain minimum level of emotional arousal to be experienced before the trapped memory is accessed. Then the trauma network of associated sensations which were formed at the time of the traumatic incident are revealed."

When, during careful debriefing, the man who survived the motorboat disaster was able to link the smell of petrol at garages with the strong smell of diesel fuel his senses had registered at the scene of the disaster, he was finally able to understand the true cause of his panic attacks. Eventually, therefore, the cortex was able to translate the sensory impressions which the amygdala had received into an understandable narrative of events. The stronger the linking of this information, the weaker the associated emotional arousal became and his panic attacks gradually stopped.

Fight or flight

I now want to explain more about this mechanism, the fight or flight response, which made such good evolutionary sense and which still has a vital role to play. Unfortunately we may be impelled to resort to the former when a more civilised approach would have been more helpful and less dangerous. Conversely, we may fail to apply the latter when we should, because of various confused forms of reasoning.

Our friend the amygdala is, as I explained earlier, our alarm system. Different parts of it control both the fight response and the flight response – and also the appeasement response. Just as a wild animal may lie on its back exposing its stomach as a gesture of appeasement to a stronger member of the species, so we too have our version. We may back off and look non-threatening. All this is under the amygdala's control and it can switch from one response to another in a flash, if deemed more appropriate in whatever the current circumstances.

What happens to get us ready for fight or flight is the same, physiologically. Our body reacts in a way that enables us to do cither of those two things. Our ancestors, if they could see a bear, would probably opt for flight. If they were encountering an unknown stranger who was smaller than they were, they might decide on fight.

It is crucial that we understand this response so that we have a greater chance of acting in an appropriate way in any pressure situation. The important thing to remember is that the physiological changes that are happening to you are also happening to your hyped up would-be assailant.

So what does happen?

- When we feel extreme fear, the adrenal glands flood the body with the stress hormones adrenaline and noradrenaline. Other parts of the brain act in sequence to trigger the production of cortisol, also from the adrenal glands. All these hormones course through the bloodstream to reach every cell in every organ of the body and gear them all up for action. In addition, the following changes also take place:

- The liver releases sugar and fats which flow into the bloodstream to provide the fuel for immediate energy

- Breathing quickens, providing more oxygen

- Red blood cells flood the bloodstream, carrying the oxygen to the arm and leg muscles and to the brain

- The heart beats faster and blood pressure rises, ensuring sufficient blood reaches the relevant areas, and creating the sensation of a pounding heart and racing pulse

- Blood-clotting mechanisms are activated in case of injury. (In the past we needed this mechanism, so that we wouldn't succumb to the first bite from a sabre-toothed tiger. However, nowadays, an increased clotting tendency may in fact cause thrombosis and lead to a heart attack or stroke)

- Muscles tense in preparation for strenuous action
- Saliva dries up and digestion ceases so that blood may more urgently be diverted to the muscles and brain. This may create a sinking feeling in the stomach. Gastric juices secreted but now with nothing to do may be felt as a burning sensation in the pit of the stomach
- Perspiration increases, to cool the body, so that body temperature doesn't rise too steeply while fighting or fleeing
- The bowel and bladder muscles may loosen
- Pupils dilate, allowing in more light, so that we can see more in the dark, should we need to
- All senses are heightened, enabling us to take swift decisions and actions.

Unfortunately for us, these physiological changes are more appropriate for dealing with the physical threats our long gone ancestors experienced in the jungles than they are for the emotional threats we more commonly experience today. A dressing down from the boss, being stuck in a traffic jam, a row with the spouse can generate humiliation, frustration or a sense of injustice but all trigger the amygdala to set in train the same physiological responses unless our higher cortex can instruct it not to.

Anxiety, excitement and fear all elicit the same responses but in differing degrees. It is the interpretation that the brain places on the experience that makes the difference. So the fluttering stomach, the heart beating a little faster, the heightened senses can gird us up and give us the edge we need to perform well in a presentation, an exam or a play or to make a bunjee jump.

Any person who undergoes these changes is in a prime state of readiness to deal with challenge, danger or other real or imaginary demands. But the state is meant to be a temporary one, reserved for extreme situations, and the body cannot maintain it as a lasting condition. Once the threat or challenge has been dealt with, the body returns to normal functioning. However, when the stressor persists (eg the bully boss, the unsatisfying job, the fear of redundancy), the body has no release and stress hormones keep on flooding the body. This is when stress is dangerous: when the build up of hormones and hormone-induced changes start acting on the body to cause illness.

This is particularly relevant here because we have been looking, in previous chapters, at the role of frustration, resentment and hostility within the workplace in exacerbating incidents of violence. Now we can see why. The organism is already under stress and may only need one final 'injustice' to be primed to lose it.

It is also worth noting that, although fight or flight is an automatic response built into our survival system, we as individuals can unconsciously 'condition' ourselves to invoke the fight or flight mechanism by our own attitudes and beliefs. For instance, if we believe that all prisoners or all mentally ill people or all black people or all white people are dangerous, we will feel threatened in their presence. This feeling of threat, though self generated, is enough to trigger the response of fight or flight. Then self justification will proceed to play a part in reaffirming our feelings. "He or she or they make me feel like this, so I am right in my assumption that they are a threat." If they then respond to our negative behaviour with their own negative behaviour, it is additional confirmation that we were right in our initial assumption about them. This is why objective reasoning and control in dangerous situations is so vitally important. Our behaviour affects others' behaviour.

Staying in control

To succeed in achieving the outcome we desire in any conflict situation, we must have the ability to stay in control. This means understanding how the operation of the primitive part of our brain – the amygdala, after all, is like a two and a half million year old monkey – and the fight and flight system can affect our own and others' behaviour. If we are dealing with an individual who is aggressive and potentially violent, we must be aware that our own actions could act as a catalyst for an escalation of their anger. Therefore the ability to control our behaviour must be a priority and our aim must be to find the safest and most elegant solution to the problem at hand without overreacting. For instance, it is no good our getting annoyed with what the other person is saying or doing and taking the issue personally. If we do this, we are not in control at all but are just reacting to the other person's actions. Our outcome, to some degree, is being prepared for us by the aggressor. And, as I said at the start of this chapter, we cannot control their behaviour but we can choose to control our responses.

Freeze!

There is one more response besides fight and flight which we may resort to when under stress. This is to freeze. You may perhaps recall a moment of such apparent terror that you felt rooted to the spot, even if just for an instance. People sometimes say things like: "I wanted to run but my legs just wouldn't move". There is a good biological reason for this.

In the report, *Killing the Messenger: the pathologising of the stress response,* mention is made of the fact that zoo-owner John Aspinall was once almost killed by an angry bear. He lay on the ground in the bear's enclosure, expecting to be about to suffer a horrible death, when he "was overwhelmed by a sudden strange sense of relief and tranquillity, and surmised that this must be some natural mechanism that enables prey animals to face painful and terrifying death". This surmise is supported by the work of neuroscientist Michael Persinger whose studies of near death experiences revealed "sublime calm and beatific visions in the face of imminent extinction".[6]

It appears from laboratory studies that becoming resigned to imminent death or undergoing enormous stress can trigger the production of large quantities of endorphins, the body's own painkillers which are far more powerful than morphine.

Trauma and pain expert Peter Levine, a former consultant for NASA whose background is in medical and biological physics, describes another function for freezing. In an article in *The Therapist*,[7] drawn from a short series in the International Journal of Alternative and Complementary Medicine, he recreates the scenario of an impala about to become the prey of a cheetah.

"Notice that the impala falls to the ground an instant before the cheetah makes contact. It is almost as if the animal has surrendered to its impending demise. But the fallen impala is not dead. Although on the 'outside' it appears limp and motionless, on the 'inside' its nervous system is still activated from the 70 miles an hour chase. Though barely breathing, the impala's heart is pumping at extreme rates. Its brain and body are being flooded by the same chemicals (for example adrenaline and cortisol) that helped fuel its attempted escape.

"It is possible that the cheetah will not be devoured immediately. The mother cheetah may drag its fallen, apparently dead, prey behind a bush and seek out its cubs, who are hiding at a safe distance. Herein lies a short window of opportunity.

"The temporarily 'frozen' impala has a chance to awaken from its state of shock, shake and tremble in order to discharge the vast amount of energy stored in its nervous system, then, as if nothing had happened, bound away in search of the herd."

Staying still is also often a human's best response to the sudden sight of certain wild animals. It is movement which attracts the attention of many animals, not stillness. It is part of survival strategy, if you can't win a fight and can't flee, to try to freeze till the threat has gone. I mention all this because it has bearing on human responses to human danger too.

Get off of my patch

Richard Dawkins, in his book *The Selfish Gene*,[8] describes an interesting experiment by the great ethologist Niko Tinbergen, which demonstrates 'territorial defence'. He had a fishtank containing two male sticklebacks. The males had each built nests at opposite ends of the tank. Tinbergen placed each male in a large glass test tube, held these tubes next to each other near the centre of the tank and watched the males trying to fight each other through the glass. Next one stickleback (I shall call it A) was moved back close to its own nest. Stickleback B was then moved into the same area. Instantly B showed anxious behaviour and appeared to be desperate to get away. From this it might first have been assumed that A was the aggressive one. Then B was moved back close to its own nest and A was put next to it there. Now, in fact, the behaviour was reversed. B defended its nest and A wanted to retreat. This is a reaction that applies as much to humans as to sticklebacks. If we think people are in our territory, we are likely to defend it vigorously. This too has lessons (to be explored in the next chapter) for averting avoidable violence.

The biology of risk

The chemistry of men's brains drives them to take risks, sometimes to the extent of endangering their lives. Why otherwise would they indulge in motor racing, climbing mountains, parachuting, canoeing round the world single-handed? Of course not all men like these sorts of activities and quite a few women do. But, in general, risk and danger appeal to men more. This, according to the authors of *Why Men Don't Iron*,[9] is because men and women have differing amounts of certain key neurotransmitters and also different patterns and numbers of receptor sites. Neurotransmitters are chemicals in the brain which allow messages to be passed from one neuron to another. Serotonin and dopamine are the two neurotransmitters with a role to play in risk.

Impulses are kept in check by serotonin. People with high levels of serotonin in the brain are likely to behave sensibly and rationally. People with low levels tend to take risks. Yes, you've probably guessed it. Men tend to have lower serotonin levels than women. As one researcher explained it: "Low levels may decrease the individual's ability or motivation to maintain self control. Low levels of serotonin are associated with irritability and tendencies toward impulsive responses to environmental conditions."

Dopamine works the reverse way. The higher the dopamine levels, the higher the risk taking behaviour of an individual is likely to be. We all need to be able to take a certain amount of risk but men, who, overall, have higher dopamine levels in the brain, are more likely voluntarily to put themselves in situations of physical danger. This can be important to bear in mind when it is men who are posing the danger to another human being – or when it is men who are charged with reacting to it.

Responding to challenge

Our fears and anxieties are balanced by our self confidence and self esteem. When we are feeling strong and positive, we are not fearful and anxious. When, however, we are presented with a threat (real or perceived) fear and anxiety increase, resulting in a drop in self confidence and also in our self esteem. Our ability to cope is challenged and so is our image of ourselves.

People whose daily routine involves effort without reward, distress and dissatisfaction are likely to experience increased anxiety and decreased self confidence and to be almost constantly in a state of fight or flight (emotionally aroused readiness). They are the ones most likely to overreact, especially if they have no active coping strategies to apply to real or perceived threats. They are a fight waiting to happen – regardless of whether they are the instigator of the violent episode or the one supposedly defending against it.

People who are unhappy and unsatisfied with their daily lives but who feel that they can do little to alter their situation are also in a perpetual state of fight or flight but are more likely to give up when in a situation of challenge, resigned to having no control over anything. This also is a dangerous response to an event which could threaten the safety of themselves and others.

How we decide to respond to threatening situations of any kind will depend on a number of factors: for instance, it may depend on what we have found effective before in similar circumstances, how we feel we are being treated at the time in question, how we feel towards the person we are dealing with and also on our social conditioning and our mental and physical abilities.

Anger, one option, is a secondary emotion. It is always preceded by feelings of frustration, humiliation, injustice or threat. It is a response to feelings. What we do know is that people who have used anger, aggression and violence in the past are more likely to use them again – especially if these means achieved their ends before. We cannot know whether this is the case, if we have not met the person before. But in many cases, we will have met the person before, had confrontations or difficult dealings with them before – and so we will have had a chance to build up an expectation of their future behaviour from past performance. (I shall be giving some guidance on that in a later chapter.)

Seeing with the brain

Historian James Burke wrote perspicaciously in his book *The Day the Universe Changed*: "It is the brain which sees, not the eye. Reality is in the brain before it is experienced, or else the signals we get from the eye would make no sense."[11] In other words, our perceptions count. We interpret what we see according to our own reality. Sometimes, hopefully more often than not, it is a constructive reality that bears a close resemblance to most other people's. But sometimes it is not. If we see what we want or expect to see – the kind of person whom we assume always makes trouble, an action we assume means something other than it does – then we are half way down the path of making trouble for ourselves.

If we put all this together and look at it in context, we can start to see what it is that so often goes wrong in conflict situations, and which leads them to escalate to violence instead of calming down.

1 LeDoux, J E (1998). *The Emotional Brain*. Weidenfeld and Nicolson.

2 Goleman, D (1995). *Emotional Intelligence: why it can matter more than IQ*. Bantam, New York.

3 Tehrani, N (1998). Debriefing: a safe way to defuse emotion? *The Therapist*, 5, 3, 24-29.

4 LeDoux, J E (1992). Emotion as memory: anatomical systems underlying indelible neural traces. In S A Christensen (ed) *Handbook of Emotion and Memory*. Erlbaum, Hillsdale, New Jersey.

5 Van der Kolk (1996). Trauma and memory. In Van der Kolk, McFarlane and Weisaeth (eds) *Traumatic Stress*. Guildford Press, New York.

6 *Killing the messenger: the pathologising of the stress response* (1998). Strex Ltd.

7 Levine, P (1998). Blowing off stress. *The Therapist*, 5, 2, 15-19.

8 Dawkins, R (1997). The *Selfish Gene*. Oxford University Press, Oxford.

9 Moir, A and Moir, B (1998). *Why Men Don't Iron*. Harper Collins, London.

10 Ellis, L (1991). Monoamine oxidase and criminality: identifying an apparent biological marker for antisocial behaviour. *Journal of Research in Crime and Delinquency*, 28, 2, 227-251.

11 Burke, J (1995). *The Day the Universe Changed*. Little Brown, Boston.

CHAPTER 6   HOW WE RAISE THE RISKS

THE MAN has been waiting in the accident and emergency department for nearly a hour. He has a gash on his head that is going to need stitching but the bleeding has long stopped. His case is clearly not one of the most urgent ones. But he is large. And he is drunk.

Several times he has barrelled up to the triage nurse, the one who assesses patients on their arrival and sets their priority for treatment, and has demanded to see the doctor at once. He is just coming up for the fifth time, pushing his way into the small room where she is assessing another patient. This time he is more aggressive. This time he picks up a scissors from her desk and starts gesticulating with it in a threatening way.

The nurse and the patient, a young woman, are terrified. What can the nurse do? It doesn't take her long to sort through her options. She reasons that she can't abandon her patients and run for it, and she is certainly not going to engage with him physically to attempt to remove the scissors from his grasp. All she can do is stop still and try to be calm. So she stays where she is. And then she does what the course she has taken tells her to do. She tries to still her thumping heart and concentrate on creating empathy with the man, establishing rapport, smiling and speaking in a soft, soothing voice.

But, as we have seen, the body doesn't work like that. Talking in survival terms, she has rejected fight; she has rejected flight and she is resorting to freeze. And she is terrified. When she tries to smile, all she can produce is that fearful expression which her amygdala instructs the primitive brainstem to conjure up at such times, to show she is no threat. The result is a strange, unnatural grimace. Her voice, intended to sound soft and placating, is trembling and cracking. Now he knows for sure she is frightened. It might make him back off, but he is more likely to want to capitalise on the fact that she knows she is in his power.

Meanwhile she is so intent on forcing her body into the recommended but currently alien body language that all her precious energy is being expended on assessing whether she is getting it right. She is so busy thinking about putting her arms behind her back, trying to stand in a relaxed manner, smiling and saying soothing things that she doesn't even hear what the aggressor is saying to her. No wonder if he ends up more inflamed, convinced he is being fobbed off and not taken seriously.

But what else is the poor woman to do, we might wonder. The problem, here, is that she thinks she has no options. It is against policy for her to leave her patients at risk. Their well-being is her responsibility, or that is how she interprets her position. We'll be having a look at that in the next chapter. Because fighting clearly isn't going to be productive, she is left only with freeze but, in the hope of building a rapport, she is trying to force actions out of herself which aren't appropriate to the freeze reaction. Nor appropriate, for that matter, to a man who is now well stuck into the fight response.

How can you build rapport with a heavy, aggressive, angry man who is the worse for drink? Rapport building is a great idea in set-ups like business transactions or the counselling room. Rapport building is about creating a bond between you and someone else, creating an understanding and a way to interact successfully. It brings results. If you like me, you'll trust me and buy my products; or be on my wavelength and support me; or trust that I'm trying to help you. It is fine stuff when you both start out on relatively equal terms and both of you are making choices. It doesn't work when you are suddenly under threat and terrified for your life. Rapport building, if appropriate, comes later.

Rapport building requires us to speak in a certain way, to gain trust and acceptance. But what the nurse isn't taking account of, and hasn't been taught to take account of, at this stage, is that her aggressor's actions are all still being controlled by his amygdala. The amygdala, remember, is the part of the brain which was last updated two and a half million years ago. It doesn't recognise verbal speech. The nurse can talk as soothingly and as sensibly as she likes but our drunk will not hear her. He is operating in a different zone.

People intent on robbing a bank or building society branch often hand over a note with their demands to the cashier instead of speaking. This may be partly to avoid their voices being heard. But it is also because they are terrified, in their highly emotionally aroused state, of getting mixed up and saying something like: "Give me the gun, I've got the money". Their actions and reactions at that point are in the control of a two million year old monkey and, at some level of their psyche, they know it. At best, they are functioning at the level of a very young child. (Young children have emotional outbursts very readily because the connections between the cortex, the higher, more rational part of the brain, and the limbic system are still weak and immature. So the signals sent by the cortex to tell the limbic system to calm down are easily overridden by the more powerful amygdala, which is fully developed from birth. That is why children act irrationally, totally at the mercy of their emotions, at times of high arousal.)

We have to remember as well that, in any threatening situation, we too at this point are being controlled by our amygdala. What we have to aim for is to be able to act in a way that is congruent with what our body is going through but which gives us a chance to switch into a higher, more rational, gear.

Our anger may make it all worse

So, we increase our risk of a situation spiralling out of control into violence if we react inappropriately at the very outset, albeit with the best of intentions. What else might contribute to the escalation into violence. I've mentioned it before and it is very important: the mental state that we ourselves are in at the time of the incident.

We may be in a state of suppressed but highly charged hostility. I referred to research in an earlier chapter which showed that a high percentage of people working in retail feel job dissatisfaction. Perhaps those who are unhappy feel they don't earn enough, that they aren't given the responsibilities or the recognition they deserve, aren't valued sufficiently, aren't looked after enough – demonstrable by lack of safety precautions and training. They may not be conscious of any of these things or they may not be able to put a name or cause to the feelings of dissatisfaction and the bodily sensations of arousal. But when an incident occurs, they may be much quicker to react in anger than they would normally have been. In other words, they overreact, although they may attempt to justify their actions and attribute a rational cause to them.

Imagine a man is trying to steal a bottle of whisky or a pair of trousers from a shop. Shop or security staff may accost him. He denies he is stealing or he just refuses to let them search him. They become more determined to bring him to book. Neither side is going to give in, so the shop staff feel justified in using a degree of force. After all, right is on their side. But is it? As we saw earlier, reasonable force does not mean any amount of force required to achieve your ends. A bottle of whisky or a pair of trousers is not worth the loss of someone's life or severe injury to their body.

What is happening here is that the defenders' actions are largely serving their own ends. They don't feel good about their employers or their place of employment. If they are among the 17 per cent who, in the Business Blueprints report cited in Chapter 2, said they took their job only because they couldn't get anything better, they probably don't care too much if their employer *does* get his stock ripped off. By laying into the would-be shoplifter, they are able to discharge some of their own hostility and aggression but attribute it to the more laudable aim of bringing someone to justice. And perhaps they even really believe that is why they are using force: "He shouldn't be allowed to get away with it." "Other people have to pay for what they have." "Why should you get it the easy way when I don't?"

It isn't just workers who are dissatisfied or uninterested in their jobs who may be at increased risk of acting wrongly in a crisis. Even when people have enormous enthusiasm for or commitment to their jobs, feeling unsupported and feeling unsafe, or feeling uncertain of what is expected, all raise the risk of unsuitable responses leading to violent outcomes in pressure situations.

People only fight to win

Another way we may unintentionally up the odds on whether a critical situation will end in violence is to create circumstances where the aggressor feels he might as well fight. It is survival instinct only to fight if we think we have a chance of winning. We increase the chances of someone thinking they can win, or might as well try it, if we *give them negative options*.

Think about the implications of the following kinds of exchanges. The ticket inspector who says to the man who has no ticket and is refusing to pay for one: "There's no way you are going to leave this train without a ticket."

The barman who says to the unruly customer: "Are you going to get out or do I have to throw you out?"

The store security manager who says to the boy who is making off with some goods: "Are you going to come back or do I drag you back?"

In none of these instances is the offer that is made to the wrongdoer likely to be appealing to them. There is no room for negotiation. So he might as well resort to violence or make a run for it, which could end in violence, or call the other person's bluff ("Okay, throw me out," or "Okay, drag me back") which again will lead to violence.

Another way to increase the risk of violence in such situations is to choose to tackle the aggressor or wrongdoer near an exit. Why? Clearly, he has a much greater chance of getting away with the goods or an act of violence if he can see the opportunity to make a successful run for it.

Let's look at the common scenario of someone in a supermarket trying to steal goods. The security officer or one of the staff notices a man concealing a bottle of whisky inside his coat. Now staff know that people can't be accused of shoplifting until it is incontrovertible that they have no intention of paying; that means that they must have passed the last point in the shop at which they might have paid for the goods; that means the till nearest the door. (In fact, many shop assistants incorrectly think they have to wait until a person has left the shop premises completely before they can accuse him of stealing.)

Let's say the man stealing the whisky is aware that a shop assistant has seen him putting it inside his coat. And the shop assistant knows the man knows he has been seen. He hopes this will make the man dump the whisky and just leave, averting any need for any action (unless, of course, he is spoiling for a fight for his own reasons).

The shoplifter, however, doesn't leave. He knows he has been seen and, when nothing is said to him, he might feel slightly more confident that he is going to get away with it. Why? Because he now believes that the shop staff are more scared of him than he is of them.

By now the shop assistant who saw him will have alerted other staff. As the shoplifter makes his way around the store or towards the exit, a few of the male staff start to congregate around the exit area, waiting to see whether he will pay for the goods or pass the last point of sale.

The thief approaches the exit. The staff see him coming. Both parties are now in an extremely heightened state of arousal. The staff are trying to look cool and professional but really they are thinking anxiously, "This could end in violence, because he is still coming!". And the shoplifter is thinking: "Are they really going to dare to try and stop me or not?"

The group of staff at the door watches as he saunters boldly through the exit. Then they spring into action, following the manager out of the shop and backing him up as he moves in front of the man. He says, as calmly as he can: "Excuse me, sir, would you come back into the store, please. I believe you have an item on you which you haven't paid for."

"No, I haven't."

"Yes, you have, sir."

"No, I haven't." The shoplifter is now edging away.

"Yes, you have, sir. A member of my staff saw you take a bottle of whisky."

"No, I put that down. Didn't like the brand."

The manager is starting to get a bit hot under the collar. He doesn't like his authority being undermined by this young man and he certainly doesn't want to look stupid in front of his staff. He feels he has to assert himself quickly.

"Are you going to come back in the store, as I ask?"

"No."

"If you don't come back, we'll drag you back in!"

Now the point of no return has been reached, literally. There is no mileage for the shoplifter in returning to the store, as the bottle of whisky will quickly be found on him. There is certainly no advantage in going for the other apparent option of being dragged in. But he is already outside the shop. He has at least a chance of escape, and that seems like his best option. So he makes a run for it.

Adrenaline is really pumping now, on all sides. The shop staff pursue him and bring him down, and if force is used incompetently or excessively, one or more of those people will end up hurt.

This is a classic scenario with a bad outcome which could have been avoided by taking a different approach.

Whose territory?

Remember the lesson of the sticklebacks. If people are on what they believe to be their own territory, they are all the more likely in any confrontation to resort to violence, if necessary, to defend it. This can be a particular problem for people in service industries who are called out to carry repairs in or around people's homes.

Employees of an electricity company, for instance, might be called out to a housing estate on a Friday evening. The problem they are there to handle first arose yesterday and the power had to be turned off for three hours, while someone worked on it. Unfortunately the causes could not be fully resolved and now the power is going to have to go off again so that the cable can be made safe while it is worked on. The new teams reckons the power will have to be off for an hour and a half.

They are out there, in the cold and rain, just about to get down to it when out from one of the houses comes an extremely irate and fit looking young man. He is swearing almost every second word. "Get the ****ing power back on, you ****ing ****ers. You were ****ing supposed to sort this out ****ing yesterday. What the **** do you think you're doing? We've got a one-month old baby in there and you're going through all this ****ing malarky again! You get the ****ing power back on right now or I'll ****ing do it for you!"

An attitude like this is not going to warm the power workers to his case. But, if violence is to be avoided, it is crucial that they *do* see that he feels he has a case. He is on home ground and he feels invaded, threatened and hard done by. His feelings are instinctive and emotionally he has much more invested in the issue than the electricians , although they, of course, have a duty and a job to do. I'll explore some of the electricians' most sensible options in Chapter 8.

"It won't happen to me"

One major reason for people becoming victims in situations that become confrontational, yet could have been avoided, is that they don't act on the evidence of others' past behaviour (if known).

Gavin de Becker, an international expert on handling threat and violence, describes at length in his brilliant book, *The Gift of Fear*,[1] horrifying incidences of individuals being enabled to commit terrifying crimes because all their past actions, that had so clearly pointed the way that they were going, were ignored. In his chapter about violence in the workplace, called Occupational Hazards, he explains "that people don't just 'snap'. There is a process as observable, and often as predictable, as water coming to a boil. Though we call it workplace violence, it is really every type of violence, committed by every type of perpetrator. It is revenge killing, when an employee who feels humiliated or emasculated proves that he cannot be taken lightly. It is domestic violence, when a husband seeks out his wife at her work. It is date stalking, when the man who refuses to let go pursues his victim at her job. It is rage killing, when an employee primed to do something big and bad chooses to do it at work. The fear of violence at work is understandable because work is a place where many of us are forced to interact with people we did not choose to have in our lives.

"Fortunately violence in the workplace offers many predictive opportunities, and there are almost always several people in a position to observe the warning signs.

Still, as the cases show, obvious warnings are frequently ignored. The cases {that de Becker cites} also show that it doesn't have to be that way."

Only very recently, there was the tragic case in this country of a 50-year-old social worker, Jenny Morrison, being stabbed to death by a man in a care in the community hostel. She had known the man; he had threatened her on previous occasions and it was known by the care authorities that he had threatened her. Yet the experienced care worker was alone with him in the hostel when he suddenly took offence at something she said and launched a frenzied attack on her with two kitchen knives.

(Incidentally, the vast majority of violent crime is committed by people who do not have mental health problems. Home Office statistics on violent crime for a year-period ending in June 1997 showed that, of 348,943 recorded offences against people in England and Wales, only 321 of the perpetrators were assessed as mentally disordered. Alcohol or drug use is a contributory factor in more cases of homicide than is a diagnosis of mental disorder. In 60 per cent of homicides committed by people with no diagnosis of mental illness, alcohol or drugs were considered to have contributed to the crime.[2])

Often people don't act on suspicion or even evidence of danger because they think they are being stupid or paranoid or impolite for feeling uncomfortable or suspicious. In other words, it is the blind belief, for whatever reason, that "it will never happen". Why do we act this way? Because we have learned to overrule one of our instinctive and most reliable reactions – fear.

Returning to the insights of Gavin de Becker, for a moment, he points out that we are much more respectful of dogs' intuition than our own. Contrary to belief, he maintains, our own intuition is far superior to that of dogs. He tells the anecdote of a friend who decided to look for another building contractor after her dog persistently growled at the one who first came to discuss the work she wanted done. De Becker explained to her that it was much more likely that the dog was picking up her own signals than vice versa. It was *she* who was dubious about his honesty, his sales talk, his over-slick approach and his guarantees. The dog would not know of such problems.

Dogs are expert at reading humans. They are loyal to us, acting on the basis that if they look after us, we'll look after them. They also sense and react to the expression of fear in a human (or animal) because that signifies danger. As de Becker points out, dogs have nothing in that department that humans don't have "but the problem, in fact, is that extra something you have that a dog doesn't: it is judgment, and that's what gets in the way of your perception and intuition. With judgment comes the ability to disregard your intuition unless you can explain it logically ... {A dog} is not distracted by the way things could be, used to be or should be. She perceives only what is."

I might, for instance, get home from work one evening after a really exhausting day and an irritatingly slow journey home through blocked traffic. My dog Rover greets me. I give him a cuddle and a pat and then gratefully get ready to settle down and relax. I've just made a cup of tea, put it beside me on the table and have my feet up on the sofa when the doorbell rings. My annoyance is palpable. Certainly the dog feels it. He rushes to the door at my side, barking furiously. He wants to protect me from this unwelcome intruder, whoever it is.

I open the door guardedly. I'm hoping it isn't someone I might have to invite in and be polite to. It turns out to be my pal Andy. "Sorry to bother you, Mark. I'll be very quick. I just wondered if I could borrow that staple gun you were going to lend me." Now Andy's a good friend and of course I'll get the staple gun for him, but I really don't feel like having to put my shoes back on and go out in the rain to the shed.

Meanwhile Rover is picking up those signals from me and is still barking loudly. When a dog barks what it is doing, in effect, is calling for reinforcements. He can't understand why I am not acting angrily, in accordance with my body language when the bell went. And I am still giving out the signal that this is an intrusion I could do without. Rover keeps rushing around my legs and towards Andy and back. He is becoming another nuisance so I put him firmly in the kitchen and shut the door.

I go out to my shed to get the staple gun. When I come back in, Rover is still barking and whining and I can hear he is scratching frantically on the kitchen door. Suddenly I remember my wife has just painted that door. Really wild now, I storm into the kitchen, grab Rover and throw him out into the garden. Then I go back to Andy, give him the staple gun, exchange a few pleasantrics, and he leaves.

Rover is completely beside himself by now. Dogs are pack animals. For Rover, I am pack leader. He wants to protect me but for some odd reason I won't let him.

Eventually, after I've calmed down again, and Rover has stopped yapping in the garden, I let him in. He is a bit hangdog and confused now. Gradually he creeps his way back into favour and we are friends again. But he thinks I'm stupid not to have let him play his part in helping to deal with the intruder.

If I'm not careful, I will very soon condition my dog not to bother to react on my behalf, if that is the response he gets. I've confused his early warning system with my contradictory actions. And of course, we often confuse our own.

In this example, the caller wasn't an intruder, although his visit did happen to be unwelcome at that particular time. However, at other times, we might do well to listen to our lower brain and not rationalise away what is happening. Between 85 per cent and 95 per cent of women are raped at home by someone they know. Sometimes the scenario might go like this.

There's a knock at the door. Carol answers it and sees Craig, her husband's best friend outside. "Hello," he says. "Is Bob in?" "No, not yet," she says. It's a funny time for him to be asking. It's only 5pm and Bob is never home before 6.30 pm. She registers the oddness of it fleetingly.

"Oh," says Craig, as if the possibility of Bob's not being there had never occurred to him. "Can I come in and wait for him?" She hesitates. The dog inside of her brain is now starting to bark. "I promise I'll be no trouble," he says. She registers these words too and they jar on her and they'll come back to her later. But she thinks she is being silly. This is Bob's best friend. For fear of being rude, she lets him in.

The signal that she is trying to ignore is telling her not to stay in the room with Craig. Perhaps she goes so far as to busy herself in the kitchen making tea, while he is in the living room, then in going in and out of the living room fetching things, like biscuits or more milk, and never quite staying put. But it doesn't do any good. Craig has come there to rape her and she has provided the opportunity, out of politeness, out of disbelief, out of not respecting and acting on her intuition.

Jill Craigie, wife of former Labour party leader Michael Foot, admitted recently that she was raped by distinguished thinker and author Arthur Koestler, a friend of them both. On the occasion concerned, not long after she was married, she and Koestler had had lunch at a restaurant together and afterwards he suggested they have coffee at her home in Hampstead. She was surprised at the suggestion, not too keen, but agreed, out of politeness. At some point, he launched a violent assault upon her. It was quite frenzied but, being young and strong, she managed to free herself and fled the house. Unfortunately, as she has described the incident, she sat, recovering, on the steps of the house and wondered what to do. She knew no one in the area, had no money on her and didn't want to go to the police, for fear of the impact of any adverse publicity on her husband's career. She sat there, expecting Koestler to come out, but he didn't. Finally she decided that long enough had passed and reasoned that Koestler must have calmed down and probably regretted his actions. So she made the awful counter-intuitive decision to go back inside. Koestler quickly renewed his attack and this time Jill Craigie was unable to fight him off.

As de Becker suggests in his book, no animal in the wild, suddenly experiencing intense fear, would ever do the equivalent of thinking, "It's probably nothing". Yet that is what we do every time we resolutely don't look behind us to check the footfall we thought we heard behind us on the dark lonely street at night. Or when we decide there can be no good reason to fear someone whose behaviour we are experiencing as menacing or odd. Or think that there must be a good reason why someone, slightly suspicious looking, went into the disabled toilet 10 minutes ago and hasn't yet come out.

Always anticipate violence. If you have a strong feeling that a situation is going to spiral towards aggression, take appropriate action.

Right methods, wrong place

It can also be an error to rely uncritically on psychological strategies which, in a different context, might indeed work effectively. Some techniques which I believe can lead to major problems when used too freely in conflict situations are those used in assertiveness training. Assertiveness training has the estimable goal of helping people put their own view clearly while taking into account the feelings of others. Assertiveness is excellent for returning faulty goods to shops, resolving disputes at work, negotiation and compromise. However, when confronted by a potentially violent individual, an assertive approach by you may be seen as aggressive by the other person. It is not only what *we* do that counts, but how it is perceived by the other person.

Suppose a young mother has just parked in front of someone's driveway. She can see their car is there, she doesn't know the people who live in the house and she hopes very much that they aren't going to want to go out in the next 10 minutes. Normally she would never dream of parking there but she is already late for picking up her son from school because of being unable to find legal parking and now she is just desperate to park the car. She decides to take the risk, run like blazes and hope she can get to the school and then back to her car without causing the occupants of the house any inconvenience.

Alas, she arrives back, with son in tow, to find the owner of the house leaping up and down, wild with rage. When he sees her and realises she is the owner of the vehicle that is obstructing his exit, he starts swearing, gesticulating and acting belligerently. A number of bad things have happened to him today and this is just the absolute last straw. But the young mother doesn't know that, of course. She has done an assertiveness training evening class and she starts to justify her actions assertively. However, with the man in the state in which he is in, governed by his two million year old monkey of an amygdala, she may end up increasing her problems.

She thinks it sounds reasonable to say something like: "I realise I've parked in your driveway and you need to go out. However I was desperate to get to the school to pick up my child and was as quick as I could be. I won't do it again". But in his aroused state, he will only hear whatever he can latch on to that confirms his right to be angry.

"Pick up your child! Pick up your child!" he might rant.

"You were the one who chose to have a child. Your child is your problem, not mine. Children are a pain in the arse!"

The trouble with assertiveness in situations where one person is incapable of being reasonable is that it depends heavily on words when words are least appropriate. Recommended assertive words like 'I', which are all about owning feelings and responsibilities, are really not so good when used in conflict situations. Saying 'I' inevitably leads to a personalisation of the issue, because the speaker is putting their personal view. If they in turn become aroused ("How dare you speak like that in front of my child!") we end up with two people who are both out of control.

Mirror, mirror

Another technique which can lead to unintended escalation of the original problem derived from neurolinguistic programming, also known, by its initials, as NLP. NLP is a means of understanding and capitalising on methods different individuals prefer to use for information processing. One of its strategies for starting to establish a rapport, which is very often effective, is that of deliberately matching your behaviour to someone else's (mirroring). When you appear to be on the same wavelength, as a result of your mirroring activities, you subtly start to alter your behaviour in the direction you would like theirs to go, and they then unconsciously start to match *you*.. So, if someone is anxious and can't keep still, you also might pace up and down before gradually starting to become more relaxed.

In the case of an aggressive person, however, the need would be to act aggressively for a short period before calming down and hoping to shift them into your calmer mode. There is a logic behind this approach. If someone is highly aroused and demanding immediate service, immediate help, immediate attention or whatever, and is met with calm, they might perceive that reaction as patronising or uninterested. They might feel as if they are banging their heads against a brick wall and could even be spurred more quickly into aggressive or violent behaviour because of it.

I believe, however, that even a brief burst of aggressive behaviour is counter-productive. It is helpful to remember that someone who is aggressively out of control is like a raging fire. A fire needs three things to keep it going – fuel, heat and oxygen. If you respond with anger, even momentarily, you are adding the necessary fuel to their fire (like adding oil to flames) and the effect is an instant escalation of anger, not a damping down.

There may be a case, at times, for mirroring signs of increased arousal: for instance, speaking loudly for a moment, simply in order to be heard, if the upset, aroused individual is talking very loudly. But that really is as far as it goes. It is dangerous to mimic actions in any way which might give the other person the impression that you are becoming emotionally involved and engaging with them at that level.

So how *should* we engage with people who are upset or angry, highly emotionally aroused and very ready either to lash out or to blame or make demands on us, as a result of their circumstances. That is the subject matter of the last two chapters.

1 de Becker, G (1997). *The Gift of Fear.* Little, Brown and Company, USA.
2 *Dangerousness and Mental Health* Fact Sheet. MIND, October 1998.

CHAPTER 7 MAKING SAFE

AN AWFUL LOT of potentially violent incidents can be deflected at the outset if we know how to take the right preventive action. Even when aggression can't be prevented, serious injury could very often be avoided if we had just taken some basic safety precautions beforehand. It is this I want to talk about now.

Simple safety measures

Taking simple safety measures means exactly what it says: not leaving around unnecessarily implements which could be seized and used to harm or threaten others. Sixty per cent of sharp implement assaults occur in hospitals or doctors' surgeries. Why? Because so often there are plenty lying around. Scalpels and other surgical tools should be kept well out of casual reach. Scissors have no place lying within grabbing distance on the reception desk at the doctor's surgery. If you arc using tools and you scc trouble coming, stow them as quickly as you can.

If your thinking is that you need to have something around with which you could defend yourself, make sure it is not in a place where someone else could get at it first and use it for the attack. And always remember, of course, that self defence only justifies the use of physical force in situations where no lesser action can be taken. Getting a fright because someone came up to your desk while you were turned the other way is no justification for hitting them on the head with an iron bar, when they only wanted to ask directions to a different department.

Put away *anything* which could be put to sinister use, even if you think of that item or implement as just one of the ordinary tools of your daily work. Learn to look with more alertness and be aware of the use to which seemingly harmless objects, like a corkscrew or a knitting needle, could be put by someone who is emotionally aroused or in a frenzy.

Build in a way out

I want you to think for a moment of your doctor's consulting room. Chances are that you walk in and either straight ahead of you or off to the side stands the doctor's desk. He or she sits behind it. There's a chair for you in front of it.

Now put yourself in the position of the doctor – maybe you are one, anyway. Or a psychotherapist. Or a lawyer. Or whoever. The position I've just described tends to feel right. You are in control, only having to raise your head to see people as they enter. But there, in fact, your control ends. If the person who has just entered starts to rage or lose their temper or grabs the scissors that shouldn't have been left out on your desk, you have no easy escape route. Your assailant is between you and the door.

If you have a back way out, okay. If not, better to position your desk at an angle to the door that enables you to get there first. It means that you are nearer to the door than perhaps you at first feel comfortable being, in that it cuts down the personal distance between you and the person entering, at the point of entry. But once they have crossed in front of your desk and sat down, comfortable personal distance is re-established and your escape route in assured.

Of course, this doesn't work if a person bursts into a room where you are alone, intent on a confrontation from the outset. Then you have to rely on the calming down measures which I shall be describing in Chapter 8.

Coordinate activities

Wherever a service is provided directly to the public, an environment is more likely to become conducive to conflict if too many different demands are put on staff at the same time, preventing them either from being vigilant or from having the capacity to deal with individuals' needs sufficiently speedily.

Who doesn't find it irritating, for instance, if everyone starts to change shift at a supermarket's customer service desk during the busiest part of the lunch time period, when queues are longest? Or if money bags are collected or organisational chits brought round to be signed by cashiers when there are many people waiting at the checkout? It only needs the previous two customers to have taken a long time packing away their goods or to have bought an item which was missing its barcode (requiring light flashing or bell ringing to summon assistance) for the next person in line perhaps to be hot enough under the collar to get abusive about any further irritating delay.

That care of this kind could be crucial in creating a safe environment is suggested in some recent research carried out in psychiatric wards. An analysis of the incident reports of eight acute in-patient wards from six districts in England over a six month period found an average of 2.5 reported monthly assaults per ward. The researchers found that the *timing* of assaults showed similarities across all wards, which surprised them. Analysis of all incidents, including non-physical aggression and self harm, showed a slow build up of incidents throughout the day, peaking in the period between midday and 3 pm. The researchers suggested as a possible explanation for the peak the fact that a number of different events coincided during a short space of time within this period: medication was distributed, meals were given out and staff changed shifts. They commented: "This was the only period when all three events occurred more or less simultaneously at the time when most patients were up and active".[1]

Prepare your (exit) strategy

You may be familiar with the saying, to be forewarned is to be forearmed. This is very true, if you choose to make it so. The only warning needed may be the sight of someone approaching who is patently not in a happy state. If that person has caused trouble before, particularly trouble of a consistent serial nature (perhaps it is someone who has come into a benefits office three days running so far, to see if his complaint has been sorted out, and is becoming increasingly angry each time he finds that it hasn't), then a very clear plan of action should be in place.

For instance, let's return to the scenario of the electricity workers who have been called out for the second day running to a housing estate and, for the second day running, are going to have to turn the power off. A resident became very angry and abusive on the first day. Now he is spotted storming out of his house again and striding towards the hole that the electricians have started digging so that they can get at a cable. It is obviously going to mean trouble. This is the time for them to implement the 'exit plan' of their strategy, which should take into consideration their duty of care to all concerned (themselves first). Remember, this situation has arisen out of their employed role and is therefore an occupational risk, so they are only required to deal with it according to the training, information, instruction and supervision that have been provided for them by their employer.

First sensible action is to make the hole as safe as possible. Somebody should be stowing away the hammers and chisels and any other tools which could be used for harm. Someone else should be starting the van. Another one should be calling the police on the mobile phone. (Perhaps, even better, the foreman has alerted the police to the fact that a problem occurred yesterday and that they might need prompt assistance today.) Anyone else should come to stand next to the foreman.

When the combusting resident arrives, spitting blood, shouting and roaring, and seizes the foreman by the arm, the electrician who phoned the police could be used as a distraction in the following manner. He could come straight over, holding out the mobile to the foreman, and say something like: "The police are on the phone. They want to speak to you about this job". This might have the desired effect of pausing the situation for a moment, allowing the foreman to withdraw – and letting the aggressor realise that the police might be getting involved.

But let's say the plan doesn't work, the man is too far gone and he throws a punch. The foreman or one of his mates may have to retaliate in self defence. (A fist, by the way, is a very weak thing to hit people with. It is just skin over bone, supported by a wrist that is pretty weak, in relative terms. Even heavyweight boxer Mike Tyson, when he hit a reporter, once broke his wrist. That's why actions of a non-physical nature are usually more successful.) As soon as the man is down on the ground and unable to scramble up quickly enough to carry on with his assault, should he want to, the team are in the van and away to the police station to report the event: "Unfortunately he assaulted me, officer. I defended myself and I've come to report the matter."

Such strategies rely on planning and leadership. Everyone needs to know their function and stick to it, unless unexpected developments call for initiative.

Sun Tzu was a famous Chinese military strategist who won numerous victories on the battlefield 2,500 years ago. His reputation still survives because his strategy was so successful that he was never defeated in battle. He has been described as the best military leader the world has ever known, and his philosophy is still taught in Asia today. The Russian military at one time used his ideas and they have also been applied to business training in America.

So what did he do? He ran his army on what is termed a 'natural organisational basis'. Crucially, it was information-centred and completely flexible and adaptable. Think of another natural organisation, for instance an ant hill or termite mound. To create that mound, termites have to work together and each plays its allotted part. No single termite has the blueprint for the termite mound in its head, yet each is essential in its contribution to creating the mound that will finally appear. This, in fact, is how, in the wider picture, companies should be run and, in the smaller frame, how safety procedures should work: everyone receiving guidance, knowing all that they need to know to carry out their role and being enabled to do whatever needs to be done in order to achieve the desired ends by desired means.

Natural organisation allows for improvisation and flexibility. There are no rigid rules, because at times rules and guidelines need to be broken. So, if one approach isn't working, it makes sense to try something else. Firemen have to use their initiative and improvise all the time, for instance, when trying to cut trapped people free or gain access to seemingly inaccessible buildings. They don't say: "It isn't in the rule book. It's not my problem." Their only concern, in what they try, is the safety of all concerned.

Don't wind people up

When people are feeling vulnerable or are under a lot of pressure, it can be all too easy to help them explode into anger by actions of our own that are guaranteed to irritate them. Sometimes people do it deliberately. Couples tend to know exactly what to say that will get under their dearly beloved's skin, if they are spoiling for a fight with them. It might be a seemingly innocent reference to a lack of financial acumen, a less than complimentary comment about the quality of a meal, a criticism of someone's tendency to swear or of someone's driving. It might be a woman's tendency to persist in wanting to sort out an particular issue when the man just wants to turn off and bury his head in the sand for a while. It might be a tendency to speak for the other person or to tidy up their things or to complain about some old established bugbear. The result may be an almost spectacular eruption of rage, which, on the surface, the situation doesn't seem to warrant.

It makes sense to avoid 'pressing the buttons' that lead potentially dangerous people to explode into rage. That sounds obvious but we don't always abide by it. A shop assistant may say in a loud aside, "Oh, here he comes, complaining again". The receptionist may say: "You'll just have to be patient". The railway worker may be told to say: "If you want to complain, write to this address".

When we are angry, we don't want to be treated as if we are regular troublemakers. We don't want to be told to be patient when we have already had it up to the hilt with waiting. We don't want to write when we are seething for an explanation or satisfaction now. Thinking about the words we use and the assumptions we make, before we make them, can avert a lot of difficulty.

It isn't just the words we use that can wind people up, it is our manner. A shop assistant may behave in an offhand way with a customer purely because she feels the customer has no respect for her or her job and she want to prevent herself feeling humiliated. By not being overly obliging, she won't feel so rejected. But the customer, of course, may not feel disrespect at all (this is the assistant's own assumption) and reads the offhandedness as contempt or lack of interest.

Pre-empt where possible

So much of the steam can be taken out of heated encounters if people act in advance to avoid their getting that hot. That means informing people and involving people, instead of presenting an unsatisfactory fait accompli.

So, in the case of the delayed train, it helps if someone announces over the Tannoy or walks through the train to explain why the delay is occurring and whether there is an end in sight. (Obviously, if the train is full of drunken football hooligans, using the public address system will be safer than walking the train.) A promise to came back and tell passengers as soon as it *is* possible to make a realistic estimate is also a worthwhile move. Of course people will still feel irritated and frustrated and let down, but they do feel informed, instead of stranded and left in the dark, and that helps to defuse the emotions. Better still is to make some offer of help, however small, that might improve the circumstances for them. "I have a mobile phone here if anyone needs to make a call to explain they are going to be late."

It might make sense for our power workers, on their return visit to the housing estate where a man was irate about loss of power the day before, to go to that man's house before starting work. By doing this they are meeting the customer on his own territory, so he will feel less threatened – but, if he does become aggressive, they must be prepared to withdraw at once. A secondary benefit is that by visiting the customer they are making him aware that they know where he lives, and that therefore, if he becomes aggressive, there is a very good chance that he will be held to account for his actions. In doing this, they are going some way towards reducing the risk of violence because it is when someone thinks that they won't get caught that the risk of violence increases.

However, when the power workers knock on the door the next day, the man may not yet be aroused. So the foreman could say: "Look, I've just heard about what happened yesterday. I'm really sorry about the inconvenience and I'm sorry that it is not over yet. I reckon it is going to take a maximum of an hour and a half for us to do what we need to do and get the power back on today." And then the offer of help. "If that's a big nuisance, can I do something to help? Can I run a temporary supply for you?"

Sometimes it is just so obvious that a word of explanation beforehand will help keep things calm. Think how often people sit for long periods in doctors' waiting rooms, seeing little movement in the traffic in and out of the consulting rooms. Appointment times are long past. Some people have to get away to collect children or meet other commitments and they are getting very edgy.

Instead of having to deal with a straggly but steady stream of increasingly cross people approaching the reception desk one by one, wouldn't it be better if the receptionist made a general announcement. "I'm awfully sorry but Dr Squires has been called out to an emergency. At this stage we don't know how long she is going to be. As soon as she lets us know she is on her way back, we will tell you. If anyone absolutely can't wait, I'm happy to make another appointment for you to come back as early as possible, if you would like to come up to the desk."

Many accident and emergency departments now display on screens or boards in the waiting area the estimated waiting times for non-priority patients. The heart may sink to see 'four hours' or 'six hours' printed up there, but at least most people become mentally geared up for the waiting, or else can make the decision not to wait or to go elsewhere.

Trust your intuition

This is a message which on Gavin de Becker puts enormous emphasis. In *The Gift of Fear*[2] he describes the 'messengers' of intuition:

"Intuition is always learning, and though it may occasionally send a signal that turns out to be less than urgent, everything it communicates to you is meaningful. Unlike worry, it will not waste your time. Intuition might send any of several messengers to get your attention, and because they differ according to urgency, it is good to know the ranking.

"The intuitive signal of the highest order, the one with the greatest urgency, is fear; accordingly, it should always be listened to. The next level is apprehension, then suspicion, then hesitation, doubt, gut feelings, hunches and curiosity. There are also nagging feelings, persistent thoughts, physical sensations, wonder and anxiety. Generally speaking, these are less urgent. By thinking about these signals with an open mind when they occur, you will learn how you communicate with yourself."

So, the act of hesitation before politely inviting in her husband's best friend could spur a woman to take seriously her risk of being raped. Acting on the suspicion that a client could have a knife could save a social worker's life. Acting on a persistent thought that a certain person is not to be trusted could avert danger. There is one other signal de Becker adds to his list, and that is humour. People who have been involved in a violent or even fatal incident may often have joked just before the event, "There's probably a bomb in there!" or "I bet he's got a knife this time!" It is a joke. That is, they feel the fleeting fear, dismiss it as ludicrous and so turn it into a joke. Something makes them voice it, but they still open the parcel or approach the knifeman anyway, instead of listening to what their joking thought is really signalling and acting on it.

Intuition often comes into play before we are even conscious of what it is that alerts us. So a woman may feel fear as she hears a male colleague enter the outer office when she is working late in her own office one evening. He comes to her door, smiles and appears to be behaving perfectly normally but, acting on her intuition, she says breezily, "Hi, Paul. Can I help you? I've just got to drop these papers into Theresa's office and I'll be back." But instead she heads straight out of the building. It is only afterwards, wondering why she did what she did, that she realises it was the closing of the outer office door, which consciously she had hardly even registered, which had alerted her to danger. There was no good reason for Paul to have closed that door.

Trust past evidence

I mentioned in the previous chapter a common failing among us to take notice of past evidence of potential or actual explosive and dangerous behaviour in someone with whom we have repeat dealings. If the man has lashed out with fists, cut with a knife or fired a gun before, he should not be interviewed alone by a probation officer, psychologist, police officer or whoever, unless instant back up is available. If the teenager has a history of assaulting children, he should not be left alone with just one other child.

When there is no previous record of violent action, we need to be able to evaluate circumstances, in the light of existing knowledge, to make a judgment about the likeliness of violence occurring.

De Becker suggests that this comes down to considering four issues: justification, alternatives, consequences and ability (JACA).

Whether a person feels justified in using violence may depend upon their perception of the situation and upon their own personal repertoire of responses. Being looked at in what someone considers a funny way could be enough to humiliate him and incite him to action. The assumption that someone has deliberately hurt or inconvenienced him in some way, when in fact it was an accident, could also be sufficient to set off a hostile response in a hostile individual. The more major the hurt or rejection or humiliation, of course, the greater the likelihood of violence. Whether an aggressive course is actually taken, however, may also depend upon whether the individual perceives themselves as having any alternatives (such as writing to the newspapers, going to court, coming up with a verbal reply to make the perpetrator of a hurt smart in turn). Perceiving only negative alternatives (as in the instance of the shoplifter with his whisky) will also make the violence option appear more viable.

Is it possible that the individual will view the consequences of being caught as being worth the violent act? Someone who has been in prison for most of their life, for instance, and who is having difficulty coping on the outside, may be more willing to commit an act of bodily harm, if for them it means returning to the one place they unconsciously feel safe, are accepted and consider their home.

The final issue on de Becker's list is "does the person believe he can successfully deliver the blows or bullet or bomb?" If someone has a gun or can get hold of a knife, they are half way there on ability. But they may not actually be able to go through with any attack. If an individual has used these means before, however, it can probably be taken as read that he would be prepared to use them again.

This is a highly useful checklist for employers or staff at management level who work in services where the clientele may pose a risk to those employed to help them.

Turn to look

If you are walking alone in a street, a corridor or any almost deserted place and you sense that someone is too close behind you, turn round. That way you identify the problem. It may be 6'4" of problem. But at least the person knows that you have courage – and that you have seen them. That may be sufficient to make them decide that the risk in mugging or sexually assaulting you is too great. You can identify them. And not everyone who commits a violent crime wants to go on to commit the ultimate crime of murder, the only foolproof way to prevent eye witness identification. Best for them to turn tail and go while they are still innocent in the eyes of the law.

The greater likelihood of meeting someone who is prepared to hurt rather than kill, to achieve their ends, definitely makes it more worthwhile to turn around than to give out to the attacker victim vibes (head down, carrying on straight ahead) which can only encourage their intended actions. All of our 'fighting machinery' – arms, legs and head – work most effectively in a forward attitude, when we are facing our opponent. If someone grabs us from behind (especially around the neck) we are at a major disadvantage. Being too scared to turn around will only heighten the trauma of an assault from the rear while reducing the ability to defend ourselves.

A 55-year-old woman whom I once taught self defence was walking home one night at 10.30 pm across a dark square of green which she was obliged to cross to reach her home. She heard a voice behind her say: "Have you got the right time?" She said she hadn't, without turning round, and walked on, feeling uncomfortable. The voice then said: "Have you any money?" She stopped. She told me afterwards that everything she had learned from me told her to turn round but her anxiety and terror said don't. She forced herself to turn around. And her would-be mugger was indeed about 6'4". She said she had never in her life experienced such an adrenaline rush before.

Raising her hands, to counter her own anxiety, she said strongly: "Go away!" He went. Perhaps she was lucky, (although technically she knew what to do if he had attacked her). More likely, by turning round, she had minimised her risk. He would rather have an easier target.

Take risks – safely

Taking a chance that a ploy will work may be a risk worth taking, if the consequences are more manageable – and more advantageous – than those of hanging back till too late.

Let me demonstrate this with the example of our young man who was trying to steal a bottle of whisky from a local supermarket. It is not the most productive approach, we saw, for store officials to wait till the shoplifter has left the premises and then tackle him. The options for him are all negative then. If he accompanies them willingly or unwillingly back into the shop, he knows the outcome. The signs on the walls say it. Shoplifters will be prosecuted. So he might as well make a break for it.

What if, however, the shop assistant goes straight up to the would-be shoplifter as soon as he sees him pick the bottle off the shelf and hide it in his coat? Most, however, would be reluctant to do this. The man can't be accused of shoplifting, because technically no crime has been committed until the man has passed the last point of sale. For there to be a case to prosecute, the assistant has to be certain of the man's intent, and he can't be certain until he has virtually left the shop. If the assistant speaks up now, all he can do is let the customer know that he thinks he is going to steal, but the understandable fear of not getting a 'nice' reply from the prospective thief may make the prospect of such a tactic seem unattractive. That's why few would want to approach the man alone and at this stage.

Yet it is exactly the time to do it. And there *is* a way he can find out the man's intent at this point without necessarily inviting himself to receive a sock on the jaw. It's a risk but it is one worth taking.

How about if he says something like this: "Excuse me, sir. Would you like a basket for that item because, if you carry it like that in your jacket, it might be thought that you are trying to steal it?"

How will the shoplifter respond? Well, he is unlikely to make a dash for it, as he is in the aisle, away from a point of exit. And he has no reason to lash out at the shop assistant because, although he now knows he has been seen in the act of trying to steal, he hasn't been accused of anything and in fact has been offered a positive alternative to prosecution: taking a basket. He might thank the shop assistant, take the proffered basket and then, around in the next aisle, dump both the basket and the whisky, cut his losses and leave the shop empty-handed.

Alternatively, he might have a lot invested in getting that bottle of whisky and be prepared to take a risk himself. Suppose he said: "You say anything to anyone, you snivelling little rat, and I'll wrap this bottle round your head".

Not pleasant to be on the receiving end of. But it is no bad thing that the man has been verbally abusive. By his abuse, he has provided a good indication of intent. So the shop assistant can now go straight to the office, call the police and tell them exactly what has happened: "When I offered him a basket to put his whisky bottle into instead of his coat, in case he was accused of intending to shoplift, he threatened to wrap the bottle round my head if I said a word to anyone." The police are duty bound to respond to a breach of the peace, which is what our potential thief was in effect promising if he was stopped when exiting the store. Also, by default, the thief was stating his intent to steal.

In fact the phone call to the police could be made by another member of staff while the first assistant is dealing with the thief in the aisle, so that there is no delay in the arrival of the police. In many towns and cities there are now direct radio links between retailers and the police to speed their response. By using initiative and taking the risk of intervening in the situation before it has got out of hand, injury may be avoided.

Such risk taking paid off for me when, during my time as a prison officer, I was asked to work with a unit that had major problems with one very big inmate who would not go back in his cell at the end of 'association period'. This was the time when prisoners were allowed to get together in the open space on the wing in front of their cells, and play pool together or watch television. The prison staff would tell him, along with everyone else, to go back to his cell and he would often refuse to go. "In your cell!" "I'm not going." "In your cell or we'll put you there!" And that, of course, is what regularly happened. The prison officers felt obliged to resort to force to manhandle him back into his cell, a consequence which the prisoner himself expected and was ready for. Although he didn't play up every single day, the staff dreaded that he might and so they were already wound up and apprehensive whenever it did happen.

I suggested we took a different approach. I suggested that, if the prisoner refused to go back in his cell, we should say, okay, and leave him there. After all, all that would happen was that he would be locked in the association area instead of in his cell. My colleagues were horrified at first. They thought it would seem as if he had got the better of us. But I managed to persuade them to give it a go with me.

The next time this prisoner refused to go back in his cell, we focused on the other prisoners until they had all dutifully filed back into their own cells and then, flanked by my colleagues, I went up to the problem inmate and asked him politely to go back in his cell. "No!" he said. He could see all of us lined up at the ready. I said, "Are you sure?", at which stage he tensed up ready for the fight that he thought was surely bound to follow. "Yes, I'm sure," he replied. "Your choice," I said and at the same time we all turned away from him and walked off. This action obviously confused him. Suddenly he wasn't in control of what was going to happen, in the way he was used to. "Hey!" he yelled. "Where are you going?" No reply. We withdrew to the office, secured the association area that he was in, and got on with our work.

The prisoner was completely flummoxed. He stormed about in the empty association area for a while, kicking at the pool table, then he decided he was fed up. There was, after all, no actual point in being in the empty area. After about 10 minutes he appeared at the window to the office. "Let me in my cell now !" he demanded. "In a minute," I replied . "No, now, you ****** or I'll ******* kill you." "Oh, I see," I said, "my motivation for putting you back in your cell is to have you batter me when I come out of the office! Not likely, mate," and I got on with my work.

Eventually I did go out of the office and into the association area to let him into his cell – when I was ready and when he had cooled off. He never refused to go back into his cell again as he had found the whole episode extremely embarrassing (we had left all of the observation flaps on the inmates' doors open, so that they could see what was going on). In short, we had taken control away from him by actually giving him what he wanted, but not giving him what he expected. It was a worthwhile risk to take.

At a later stage, when I was talking to this inmate, I asked him why it was that he had never gone into his cell when he was asked by staff. He told me that it wasn't that he didn't want to go back in – he just didn't like the way in which he was asked. I expect he was probably asked in an offhand way because staff were scared or intimidated by him. To try and reassert a sense of control, they had then resorted to physical force. Not a good strategy.

Get out!

When I am running training courses, I say to people that if they find themselves in a situation where violence seems inevitable, my first advice to them is to leave it. Get help if necessary, but never try to handle a situation on your own. This is where people always respond: "But I can't

just leave! What about my patients/clients/customers?"
And so my next question to them is: "By staying, what
exactly is it that you are doing to help them?"

I once did a training course with library staff who were
having enormous problems with adolescent boys who kept
coming into the library and pulling the books off the
shelves. "We confront them, and they just get worse," they
moaned. "Why not leave?" I asked. They were horrified.
They couldn't do that. They saw it as their responsibility
to protect the library and the users of the library. How
could they walk out and leave elderly people alone in there
with those boys?

They accordingly didn't. But what *did* they do? They
tried to stop the boys and inevitably one or more of the
library staff got hurt.

I told them that anyone in such a situation risks
increasing the violence by staying. Don't try vainly to
protect the books, I said. Walk out into a back room or
walk out of the library altogether, if necessary.

It is helpful to remember what I said in an earlier
chapter about someone who is aggressively out of control:
they are like a fire that needs fuel to keep it going. If you
respond with anger, you are adding the necessary fuel to
that person's fire. But if you are calm, denying the fuel,
the situation has to burn out. The boys hurling the books
soon lost interest when no one was present to challenge
them.

Always be ready to leave, if you are in a situation which
you assess as definitely about to get out of hand. Never
mind the confidential records, never mind the paperwork,
the wallet or the handbag. You may be talking survival.

Just get up and leave if that is what you have to do. In
most instances, however, it is better to leave without its
being obvious that you are effecting an escape, if you
can. You might say: "I think I've got something that might
help you/ might explain this. I'll be straight back". Or

"the supervisor has authority to deal with this. I'll go and get her immediately". Or "I'll go ring for the consultant surgeon to come down at once". Then go.

In many cases, it might be okay to come back, and it can be a useful tactic to do so. I shall be exploring that in the next chapter.

For the purposes of this one, the point I am making is that no one is obliged to put their life on the line for the sake of protecting their employer's property and it isn't wise to put it on the line for the sake of protecting your own either. If it is clear that the assailant cannot be reasoned with or reached in any way, you can do far more good for anyone left behind if you rush to summon immediate, effective help.

Let us consider a situation a nurse on an accident and emergency department could encounter. In many cases, as already mentioned, the risk to nurses is higher than in most other occupations. What if a nurse is confronted with a knife wielding aggressor, who has momentarily lost control?

Firstly let us consider the knife. One of this country's leading authorities on edged weapons, Inspector Peter Boatman, has collated a number of unnerving facts for a report produced for his police force, Northamptonshire Police. For example, edged weapons are the most commonly used instruments for killing people (used in seven out of twenty homicides.[3] In half of all muggings on men, the offender is armed with a sharp instrument such as a knife or a screwdriver.[4] A study carried out in 1983 by Dennis Tueller, a sergeant in Salt Lake City Police Department, showed that a man armed with a knife could close a gap of 21 feet and deliver a fatal thrust in about 1.5 seconds. Recent figures from the health workers' union, UNISON, show that over a 12 month period 70 per cent of ambulance workers have been the victims of violence, with weapons used in a third of all incidents. Of the 46 per cent of staff nurses who have been victims of violence, six per cent were attacked with weapons.

Secondly, let us consider the mind set of a nurse. Nurses are caring people and no one enters the nursing profession for the money, although of course they should receive far more pay than they actually get. It is the career or vocation that is the attraction. Nurses are there to preserve life, the life of others.

Thirdly let us consider the accident and emergency department environment. People in pain will obviously be less tolerant than those who are not. As a result of the time they may be expected to wait on a busy evening, they will also be frustrated and impatient.

So if a nurse is working late on a Friday evening and a drunk or someone on drugs is in the queue for treatment and has been waiting a while, she already has a potential problem. Add to that the number of 'edged weapons' that are to be found in and around accident and emergency departments and we have the potential for a fatal catastrophe.

The drunk becomes aggressive and either grabs a sharp implement or produces a knife from his pocket, brandishes it at the nurse, and screams at her in threatening and abusive language. He smashes a trolley up by throwing it on to the floor. The nurse might think she ought to try and reason with the knifeman or even try to disarm him, for the sake of her patients, but we have seen earlier that this is unlikely to work and, if she is not physically competent to engage with the assailant, her most sensible options are either to withdraw or go.

By withdrawing I mean getting some kind of barrier between herself and the knifeman as quickly as possible. (Remember just how quickly an armed individual can move.) This barrier could be a treatment trolley, for example; the aim being to prevent the attacker from breaching the physical space between himself and the nurse to deliver the weapon strike (it is extremely rare for an attacker to throw a knife). Once this safe space has been created, it might be possible for the nurse to work on calming the man. If, however, the assailant is intent on causing her harm and tries to remove the barrier – or if there isn't a barrier she can use at all – she should leave the area altogether. There is absolutely no point staying to do anything more in a situation where an individual is completely beyond reason and may possibly injure someone seriously or even fatally.

The need for physical force in this situation could now be highly likely, not for disarming the assailant or controlling the knife hand, but to help the nurse survive the encounter and make good her escape. The amount of force that would be deemed justified in such a situation is likely to be extreme and potentially dangerous. Peter Boatman, in his report, raises the following issue: "When the hierarchy of weapons is examined, most experts worldwide agree that the progression of deadliness is from baton to knife to gun. If this is the case, then why should police officers attempt to control a knife wielding attacker with a lower level of force?" A nurse, by definition, would have received less restraint training than the average police officer and be equipped with less protective equipment. So it would be reasonable for her to make use of any item in her immediate proximity for her personal protection – for instance, a fire extinguisher, walking stick, metal bar, chair, or anything else that she can lay her hands on.

I want to make it be absolutely clear at this point that I am talking about self defence – staying alive, not control of a dangerous individual. If this nurse tries to engage her knife wielding attacker 'nicely' she will undoubtedly fail.

At a seminar in London last year I was highlighting this point when a woman in the audience took exception to it. She stated that what I was saying was not acceptable. Nurses should not consider going to such extremes. When she had finished another woman stood up, rather shakily and obviously upset. In spite of her nervousness, she thanked me for the advice but said she only wished it had come 12 months earlier. She had just returned to work after an extended absence. Earlier that year, in her hospital, someone had attacked her with a knife and had plunged it into the back of her head. She had tried to stay on the scene for the sake of her responsibilities, as she perceived them, but the only result was that this brave woman's life was, in an instant, turned upside down.

Report the problem

If staff experience any problems with procedures laid down for safety, or find that things just don't work according to the rulebook, or that there is no back up when there should be or that any other consequences just haven't been thought through (nurses being obliged to stay on duty after a violent incident, for instance, or not being offered support till weeks afterwards) *they must report it.* In fairness, management cannot act if they don't know there is a problem. Proper reporting structures need to be implemented and staff should be actively encouraged to report all incidents of violence.

It needs be made absolutely clear to management just how widespread such problems are (an isolated incident is easier to ignore), so that they know they must look at innovations or modify procedure. If the same sort of incident happens again and again, report it again and again. The worst response is to get into a state of learned helplessness about it, cease to react and just become stressed and ill and demoralised and frightened. Stay on the case. Persistence is what may be needed, to precede change.

All right, so it looks bad statistically when reports show an increase in incidents, but how else can the true extent of the problem be determined? If it is known, then physical security measures, safer working practices and training can be specifically targeted, and measured for effectiveness in reducing the risk and eliminating the problem.

I do know, however, that staff in many organisations do not trust their employers. I know of one organisation which has adopted a 'zero accident' culture. The aim, obviously, is to reduce the risk of staff accidents at work to zero. However, this is being achieved by staff being encouraged *not* to report incidents, and by bringing back sick / injured staff within three days, so that no accident need be reported under RIDDOR regulations. This may look good on the balance sheet, but is utterly immoral. Staff, however, go along with it for fear of reprisal at work – bullying and intimidation. One member of the staff of a large company said that management had told them: "If you don't come back, we'll get someone else to". Should any member of staff be seriously injured as a result of this appalling denial type approach to safety, I should hope that the full weight of the law would fall on those in management found to be responsible for such illegal and immoral practices.

1   Warren, J and Beadsmoore, A (1997). Preventing violence on mental health wards. *Nursing Times*, 93, 34, 47-48.
2   de Becker, G (1997). *The Gift of Fear.* Little, Brown and Company, USA.
3   Home Office Research Study 89, *Personal Violence.*
4   British Crime Survey 1992.

Chapter 8   Calming, relating and managing

Most people don't set out to hurt others. It is when a client or customer gets upset because they don't like waiting or don't like the bill they've received or feel an injustice has been done to them or that they have received poor service that the problems usually start. In other words, it is the nature of the interaction between people that can increase the risk of violence. And it is what happens next that will decide whether the problem is sorted out peaceably or not.

I always tell people that whoever controls the interaction controls the outcome. Unfortunately many people start interacting – whether by trying to reason with the unhappy individual or by squaring up to them – before they have even established in their mind what they want their outcome to be. They react, and then they are at the mercy of circumstances. But if they know beforehand their desired outcome and interact in a way most likely to achieve it, they are more likely to become the master of the option. In situations like these, the desired outcome should always be the same: a *safe* resolution of the issue at hand. Please note the stress on the word 'safe'. When a store manager tackles the would-be shoplifter, his aim should not be to recover the goods at all costs (often the cost being an arm or a leg or a life) but to intervene in a way that takes account of the right of everyone involved to safety.

There are many steps we can take in conflict situations to help us calm the situation down and prevent it 'going off' completely. It is these I want to explain now.

Stay in control

This first one is not an option. It is an essential in every encounter involving conflict. I've mentioned the importance of staying in control before and it is so vitally important that I am going to discuss it again now. It is so important because it is the very first task for anyone who is hoping to defuse a potentially violent situation. If you lose control of your own responses at the outset, you may have given up the chance to control the situation at all and you will probably be acting in a way which will inflame your assailant or aggressor further. Always be aware how their behaviour is affecting yours and how yours is affecting theirs. If you are not in control, then who is?

To stay in control, you must be aware of that monkey bit of brain, the amygdala, which is sending out alarm signals like crazy and urging you into fight, fight or freeze mode (and your aggressor into fight mode). You can't ignore or deny this activity in the brain, but you can take steps to make it work *for* you instead of against you. Just knowing that your own brain is in this aroused state and encouraging you to act instinctively is a start. You can then take conscious steps to switch out of it by creating a different meaning for yourself about what is happening. Instead of concentrating on any personal affront and feeling personally aggrieved, you can respond from a different standpoint.

I'll illustrate my meaning with an instance that may be familiar to quite a number of readers. Let's say that I am driving along in my car through a very busy section of town. There is a lot of traffic and everyone is looking for the shortest way through. In such situations, there is always a fair bit of cutting in. I'm probably doing it myself if I get the chance. But if it happens too often to *me*, I'm going to start fuming. I start fuming. I'm getting into the mood now where I'm expecting aggressive driving and I've had my fill of it. Physiologically, my body is now gearing up for a fight. Yet another car slides in front of mine just enough to stop me going forward in my own lane of traffic without hitting it. I'm seething! I'm incandescent! And then, as the driver in front cheekily turns to wave, acknowledging me for 'letting' him in, I see to my astonishment that it's my neighbour, the nice chap who lent me his lawn-mower when mine broke down. What a surprise to see him here in this part of town! I wave back.

My whole mood has suddenly shunted into a different gear because now I have information. Whereas before I saw myself in self defence mode, in circumstances where I expected everyone to have ill intent towards me (ie, they'd seize every chance to get into my territory, my lane), suddenly my expectation about the latest interloper is different. He's my pal. He doesn't mean to harm me. Yes, come on in front of me, old boy, no problem, I'm happy to help you out, just like you helped me out with the lawn-mower. My cortex, using the information it has access to, has successfully told my amygdala to back off.

We *can* switch into a different gear, once we choose to interpret an incident differently. Whilst engaging in this process there are also a number of physical things we can do to enhance our aims.

Step back, hands raised

If, however, we are in a frightening situation where our instinct is not to fight but to flee, we can't talk ourselves out of fear by trying to tell ourselves that the 6'6" aggressor in front us, wielding a knife, is just going to cut himself a slice of cake from the kitchen. We have to respect and work with the fear that we are feeling.

What do we instinctively want to do if someone is threatening us, invading our personal space? We want to step back. And we should do so. There is absolutely no virtue in standing your ground, trying to look unconcerned or strong. Your body just doesn't believe you and it will betray your fear in a squeaky voice or a trembling hand. Take one step back. The set moves in every single form of martial arts start that way, with one step that transfers the weight on to the back leg. Doing that makes you feel slightly safer yourself and you are also giving the signal that you intend no aggression.

Increasing the space between yourself and an enraged individual is a very good option to consider for a number of reasons. First, safety. If we are too close that may be seen as threatening by the aggressor. Distance is also a benefit in the transmission and reception of information between the amygdala and the higher brain centres that put a damper on its emotional outbursts. We know that the path from the thalamus to amygdala takes thousandths of a second to traverse, which stimulates quick responses in threatening situations, but the damping down of those initial signals takes longer. By increasing the space between ourselves and the aggressor we allow time for signals from the higher brain to reach us before we act, thereby reducing the risk of an assault taking place.

Imagine, for instance, a husband and wife having a blazing row. They are standing inches away from one another, certainly within striking distance. The amygdala, in both cases, is lit up like a Christmas tree, hijacking the higher, more rational brain. The wife, in a state of heightened emotional activity and sheer frustration, slaps her husband who responds with a punch, sending his wife flying across the floor to rest in a bruised and bloody heap six feet away from where the punch took place. Immediately he says he's sorry. He has hit the very person he loves the most in a state of overreaction and heightened emotional arousal. The monkey has had its fight, which, for the sake of moving a few feet away, could perhaps have been avoided.

Protect yourself

The courses that go on about creating rapport and using body language may tell you at this point to put your hands behind your back. This also has the virtue of conveying to the aggressor that you don't mean to fight. But hang on, here. If someone is coming at you, what is the instinctive reaction? To raise the hands to protect the face or upper body, of course. Think of it as part of our basic survival strategy. The mind can operate without the body but the body cannot operate without the mind. The need to protect the head, therefore, is vital; hence hands up, not hands down.

It is also impossible to force ourselves, when terrified, to stand with our whole fronts exposed, hands behind our back, and expect ourselves to come out with a commanding voice when we speak. More natural, to give ourselves at least a chance of sounding congruent, is to raise our hands firmly to around chin level, palms straight up and facing our aggressor, and speak from this stance. The position I am describing is a placatory one but not a victim one. It is not a cowering, with fingers curled. It is a strong act that, in effect, says to the other person, "stop a moment!" It shouldn't rile them, but at the same time it serves your own need to raise your arms in self defence. From this more protected position, it is possible to produce a strong and calmer-sounding voice, instead of one that cracks with fear. You don't want your aggressor to know you are really scared. If they think you are scared, they may be more likely to resort to violence because they think they can win.

Walk away, purposefully

We might, in certain conflict situations, be able to walk away for a moment, to defuse the negative power in the confrontation and to give time for our brain to send out calmer signals.

For instance, a ticket inspector walking the carriages on a London Underground train, is likely to find someone somewhere who refuses to show him his ticket. (Tickets, by the way, aren't usually shown at barriers by the exits to stations any more, because that is too close to an escape route and encourages fare dodgers to think they have a chance of making a successful break for it. So tickets are inspected where there is no immediate opportunity for ticket evaders to escape – on the train.)

Our ticket collector approaches a seemingly respectable looking man who is sitting in the carriage and asks politely: "May I see your ticket, sir, please?" "No." "May I seek your ticket, please?" "No!" "If you don't have a ticket, you will have to pay a £10 penalty fare." "I am not showing you my ticket."

This is test time. The ticket inspector knows everyone else in the carriage is watching. He has his dignity and his professional pride at stake. The amygdala has swung into action by now. He thinks, "This bloke's not going to get away with this!" He steps closer. If he says something unthinking like: "If you don't show me your ticket or pay up, I'll put you off this train!", he may have cooked his goose. He has offered two negative alternatives and, if the man decides to call his bluff, he may feel forced to act. From all that we know of customary behaviour on the London Underground, other passengers will not necessarily come to his assistance, should things get nasty.

If, however, the ticket inspector *at this point* realises he is not on to a winner, he may decide against what will become a violent encounter and leave the situation. But he himself will be seething inside and wishing he had killed the guy. In other words, all the fight or flight hormones will still be coursing through his body, with nowhere to go. He feels defeated and hostile and it is his own health that will bear the brunt of that.

Better if the ticket inspector had walked away when the passenger refused the second time to show his ticket, *before* giving him any negative alternatives. The problem now, though, is what is he going to do next. If he just turns away from the first passenger and moves across to the other side of the carriage (creating distance), asking to see another passenger's ticket, the second passenger may well think: "Hey, wait a minute! I've paid £60 for my monthly travelcard and that guy gets away free! I'm going to refuse to show mine too". So he says to the ticket inspector: "I'm not showing you my ticket, if he's not!" At least that is what the ticket inspector may think. In reality many passengers will say absolutely nothing after witnessing such an incident.

It is very important that the ticket inspector knows how to deal with the second person. He needs to disengage from the first man and behave in a way that will help his own fight response to calm down but to do that he must be able to act effectively on the situation and take control, otherwise he may end up humiliated by refusals from everyone. He needs to speak confidently: "I can assure you that we don't have a problem, sir. We are dealing with this as we speak. Could I please see your ticket?" It is likely that he will be shown it.

Having moved around a few other passengers, he should be calm enough to come back to the first man. It is possible that, because the ticket inspector didn't take him on, the first man will now decide to show his ticket. Many passengers who initially refuse to show their ticket actually have one. Some might refuse to show it as a way of expressing their dissatisfaction with what they view as a poor service (perhaps the train was delayed). Some might just have had a bad day. Refusing to bow to the system once is often enough to discharge their temper and they usually produce the ticket when asked again, albeit with a show of resigned defiance – "Oh, there you are, then".

Inform, don't threaten

But then there is the small percentage of people who don't show tickets, who say, when asked again: "No! I told you once. Now **** off!"

Should the ticket inspector get heavy? Should he walk away, feeling humiliated and hostile? He doesn't need to do either. He could say courteously but firmly, while keeping a polite distance from the passenger concerned: "Sir, if you get off this train without a ticket, there may be another revenue inspector at the barrier and, possibly, the transport police and you may be arrested". If the man still refuses to show his ticket or pay for one, the ticket inspector can now just walk away from him altogether. He doesn't have to feel humiliated, because he has set out the possible consequences for the man and the man has merely made his choice. He can indeed radio ahead when the passenger is leaving the train and describe what he looks like, so that rail staff or railway police can be waiting for him. He has not abandoned his duty nor lost his dignity. He has not even appeared ineffectual, because all he set out to do was offer information, which he has done, not make threats that he couldn't carry out. What he has not done, quite simply, is risk his life for the sake of £10.

Don't take it personally

When dealing with someone who is out of control and extremely angry, personalising the issue always raises the risk of violence.

Even if the aggressor calls you a yellow livered toe-rag for not organising his social security payments as he wanted or for not letting him go to the front of the queue, you are just the anonymous tool of his misfortune, as far as he is concerned. So don't respond with the classic "don't you dare talk to me like that!" or "who do you think you're talking to?" Commands and questions of that nature invite the aggressor to warm even further to his subject. "I'll talk to you any way I like, you ****ing ****ing piece of ****." Or "why, who do you think you *are* then, you ****ing ****ing piece of ****?"

It is certainly important not to appear to be a faceless representative of the system, who can be abused and attacked on its account, but you do that by the reasoned and helpful way you later respond to the problem at hand, not to the insults. Don't try to sort out their attitude. Stick to the problem.

Let them vent

If you are facing someone who is enormously angry, justifiably or not, about something you have or haven't done, but you have assessed that it is safe not to leave, and more importantly you are not losing your calm, just let them vent their anger for a while.

Remember that the enraged individual may have certain negative expectations about you. They may distrust authority or feel frightened and intimidated by the fact that you represent a particular organisation. Even if your work involves caring for people, the knowledge that you belong to a large organisation and the fact that you wear a uniform may be enough cause for them to have such feelings towards you.

Take your step back, raise your hands as I described above, if you feel threatened, but otherwise just listen. You must *really* listen to him. Show you are listening by murmuring words like "mm" and "I see". Paraphrasing to yourself, every so often, what he is saying can help you keep your attention on his words and not on what you think about them or him or his behaviour.

Now is not the time to try to break in and talk yourself, to explain that others have been waiting as long as he has or that the deliveries were delayed because of some problem with the computers last week. *He cannot hear you!* Remember, his amygdala is in full charge, driving the show, and it is a monkey that cannot understand language. Even if the occasional word does get through, he is not interested at this stage in whether other people have to wait or whether your computers are messed up. He is only interested in his own experience of the problem. If you keep interrupting, he might seize you by the throat in fury and roar: "You aren't listening to me!" And he would be right.

Let him vent until he has said all he needs to say. When someone is still in the act of shouting at you, they are not actually a threat to you and you are getting important information. Also, venting will help to cool him down. You cannot do anything at all towards solving or ameliorating the problem situation until he has calmed down.

Be ready to leave

Always, always, be ready to leave a situation if you are physically able to. Sometimes, if the venting seems to be going on too long or the temperature is escalating instead of cooling, it can help the situation if you go out of the room on some pretext and then, if you judge it safe, return after some minutes. "I'll just go and check in the records next door". "I think I have some paperwork that can help us here." While you are gone, it might be that the person's ire starts to cool, with nothing to fuel it, and he becomes calm enough to listen to *you*. If not, and your unreasonable client or customer or patient looks prepared to blow up again, be ready to repeat the escape procedure. "I'm awfully sorry. I just wanted to let you know that it's not where I thought it would be. I'll be back in a moment. Would you like a cup of tea?"

It is, however, important to understand here that individual control is important and, as with all of the issues dealt with in this chapter, it is important to make your own style work for you. Mechanically driven tactics will come over as false and will soon be seen for what they really are. You must feel comfortable and natural with what you are doing.

Sometimes, giving a sudden clear instruction can be helpful. You are probably familiar with the stage hypnotist's ability to make subjects perform an action just by suddenly issuing a command. The brain, in its trance state, responds unquestioningly to the instruction. Well, a person who is consumed with anger is also in a trance state. They are oblivious of everything else. But you can often get through to them by the same means, the sudden command. The aggressor, confused and disoriented by his own heightened emotions, responds automatically to an unthreatening but forceful command, such as "Take a seat! I'll be back in a moment". (This is a particularly good one to try because the act of sitting down, not pacing and gesticulating, may help take the heat out of the situation while you are absent.)

Don't walk out without explaining where you are going, if you are intending to come back. That's a bit like leaving people on a stopped train fuming and getting angrier as they wonder why no one is telling them the cause of the delay. You don't have to say anything very informative, in this instance, however. You just need to give the impression that something productive is happening.

Our electrician foreman who was accosted by the angry man on the housing estate when he was about to turn off the power would probably find it impossible just to turn away while the man was in full flow, without saying something to explain why. He would get a response like: "Hey! Where the **** do you think you're going?" and might well receive a restraining hand or boot. But he could cut in firmly mid-flow with a direct order like: "Wait there a second! I'll be right back!". And he has then bought himself permission to leave.

I have used this technique innumerable times myself, to calm an escalating situation. Once was when I was a prison officer, working in a wing for young offenders and young remands. I was in the unit office, in charge for the day, when an inmate burst in. I'll call him John. He was 21, huge, and a fanatical weight trainer. He was fuming because he hadn't had a chance to go to the canteen. The lads were allowed to go only once a week and he had been in the gym when the prison officers running the canteen had rung us to say they were ready to take our wing.

When John came back and found he had missed his chance to go and buy his weekly chocolate supply, he was mad. But I didn't know any of that. All I knew about it was that he came in to my office f-ing and blinding, nostrils flared, fists clenched, banging walls and absolutely ready to erupt completely.

It was quite clear that, whatever I had tried to do, it wouldn't have pleased him. He wanted a fight. I said: "Tell me the problem. I can't help unless you tell me." He started ranting then, describing in graphic detail what he would like to do to me and my colleagues.

I got up, said forcefully, "Hold on! I'll be back in a second!" I went out of the office from the back and phoned for a control and restraint team to stand by. When I returned, I said: "I'm sorry about that. What's the problem? You were having a go at me." If he had started again, I would have said: "I'll be back in five minutes!" and I'd have left once more. And I would have come back again and left again, each time telling him what I was doing – in effect, keeping him posted, although nothing was happening.

But, as it turned out, he had had long enough to cool his heels the first time I went and, with no one to bounce off against while he was alone, he had calmed down. So much so, in fact, that he apologised. He explained how upset he was to have missed his chance to go to the canteen. So I picked up the phone again and said, instead of a control and restraint team, could I have someone to take John to the canteen to buy what he wanted. And he got his Crunchie bars and was happy.

Say sorry

Once a situation has started to simmer, people are often reluctant to go for the simplest remedy – apologising. On my courses, if I suggest people do this, they don't like it. If you are in the wrong (the young mother who parked in front of someone's driveway, for instance), it makes sense to say: "I'm sorry. I'll move my car right now", rather than start reacting to the rude comments being made about us. This immediately deprives the ranter's fire of fuel. He may come back with: "Oh, it's a bit late now, young lady", but that sounds a bit lame and it will be hard for him to keep up the head of steam he started with.

Whoever is 'right', always be prepared to take the blame, in some form, rather than defend yourself. Better to say something like: "It's totally understandable that you feel this way" rather than, "well, it's certainly not my fault".

Watch the body language

Ninety-three per cent of communication is non verbal. That means only seven per cent of what we communicate depends upon what we say. And, if the person we are trying to communicate with is highly emotionally aroused, we can cut that seven per cent down to two per cent. As I mentioned before, when a person is out of control, that is not the time to talk. It's a case of 'don't tell me, show me'. And what we show is therefore very important.

I have already explained why it is inappropriate to aim for relaxed friendly body language when you are terrified. Hands behind the back, for instance, apart from being a vulnerable posture to adopt, also signal that one is trying to restrain one's behaviour. In this case, the user is trying to restrain their fear but what it may convey is an attempt to control retaliatory aggressive feelings. Remember the 'step back with hands raised, palms up and open' drill, if you are being threatened.

If you do not feel directly under threat, it is just as important to use your body language appropriately, to avoid the risk of antagonising the other person. We don't like our personal space invaded, so don't enter theirs without permission. Don't stand in a way that could be considered provocative. For instance, a nonchalant slouch, with hands in the pockets, could signal a lack of respect or interest. (Hands in the pockets can also signal an attempt to restrain one's behaviour.) Standing feet apart and with hands on hips or arms folded can communicate superiority and belligerence. Standing square on, with your feet pointing straight at their feet, is aggressive. Also, do not maintain unbroken eye contact for long periods, in the belief that this communicates interest and concern. Most people find it unnerving to be looked at too long. Some may find it threatening. Do make (and break) eye contact, as appropriate, however, otherwise you may be conveying fear or, again, disrespect.

It is wise to try to read the body language you are on the receiving end of, too. If the hand comes up in front of the mouth, it is often an unconscious act that signifies lying (children do it). And if an aggressor stops blinking and proceeds to stare, it could be an indicator of very imminent violence. Stopping blinking means a person is deeply in a trance state, where they are totally absorbed in their own intent or actions. In a survey of prostitutes, in which they were asked what danger signals alerted them not to get into a car with certain punters, one of the main ones mentioned was unblinking eyes.

Avoid making any jerky movements which could be misinterpreted, such as suddenly reaching for something without warning, which an attacker might construe as your reaching for a weapon. Trauma care expert Noreen Tehrani describes one case in which a woman bank clerk was shot by a gunman in a hold up because, in complying with his demands for the money, she bent to move her chair which was in a position which prevented her opening her cash drawer. The gunman thought she was going for a panic button.[1]

When we communicate we emphasise certain points by gesticulating with our hands and arms. This gesticulation serves a very important purpose. It allows us to express the emotion designed to accompany the verbal information we provide, thus emphasising the intensity of whatever it is we are attempting to communicate. (If we are too close, incidentally, we may actually not see such gesticulation, or, even worse, mistake a sudden movement as a threat instead of what it was intended for, and react in a manner designed to eliminate a threat.) When people gesticulate they give us a glimpse of what it is that is really troubling them. As Gavin De Becker puts it in his book *The Gift of Fear*, they throw out satellites which beam back information that we can use at a later stage. What these satellites do is to give us a glimpse of what lies beneath the surface. All behaviour is the expression of a need, so even un-reasonable behaviour must have a reason. An aggressor may feel the need to resort to such an extreme form of communication simply because they believe that otherwise you would not have listened, because you don't care, aren't interested, etc, which may have been their experience with other people in authority, or stem from the fact that they have negative and uncertain expectations about you. If we are staying to solve a problem, then we need to identify what the problem is. So if an angry person suddenly starts gesticulating while mentioning their child, for example, we have just been given a glimpse of what lies below the surface. There may be a problem with one of their children, but don't jump in yet. Remember and wait.

Don't humiliate – but don't be frightened of humiliation

The last thing you want is to humiliate someone who is already hyped up and spoiling for a fight. Suppose a man who has clearly had too much to drink comes up to the bar in a pub and asks for another whisky. The barman may say "No, you've had enough". The drunk may then become aggressive. "Give me another one, do you hear!" It obviously isn't a good idea for the barman to say: "Are you going to leave or shall I throw you out?" (negative alternatives) but is this a good place, in public, for the barman to tell the man that he will call the police?

His aim is to get the man out of the pub without a violent incident. He might do better to say, "Okay, have a seat and I'll bring your drink over". When he brings it over he can say, in private: "This is your last one. If you ask for another, I will have to call the police, as it is my licence that is on the line, here". The drunk can have his drink, leave and also save face. He has got what he wanted, but so has the barman – who has probably calculated that one more whisky for a man who is already drunk is neither here nor there, if he can use it to bring the incident to a successful conclusion. (If, however, the drunk is known to be driving, the barman could offer to call him a taxi and inform him that the police are doing spot checks on drunken drivers in the local vicinity.)

When you are the one at risk of feeling humiliated, it is important to keep in mind the outcome you are after – not your intact pride but the safety of yourself and others. By the way you handle the incident, and by not being preoccupied with the need to avoid public humiliation, you are likely to achieve both ends anyway.

After calming comes relating and managing

Only when you have managed to calm someone down should you think about trying to establish a rapport with him and sorting out the issue at hand. But don't throw away all you have managed to achieve so far, once he is calm, by assuming the moral high ground and saying something like: "Right, I'm going to try and see if I can help you. But if you ever do/try anything like that again, I'll ...!"

Do, however, empathise and concentrate on helping the person not feel bad for losing his temper. When we let off steam and yell at someone, we may feel good at the time, we may feel vindicated briefly afterwards ("There, that's shown him!"), but pretty quickly we may start to feel a bit foolish for losing control. So there's no harm in showing empathy, perhaps saying something like (according to the circumstances): "Don't worry, mate. I lost my rag like that yesterday, with the missus. I didn't mean to but it just happened"; or "Don't worry, I lost my cool only yesterday, myself".

Empathise in any way you can. How can I empathise, you might say, with someone so unlike me in every way? But, of course, they are not unlike you. Somewhere, in the gamut of human emotions, there is common ground. Capitalise on it. Maybe a person has lost their cool because they have had to wait too long or they feel they have been treated badly or they are frightened about the possibility of something negative happening (losing their job, having the power cut off, losing their benefits, losing some right). We all know those feelings, even if in different circumstances and even if we would not have reacted in the same way to them.

Show you were listening

Go back to something they mentioned when they were ranting and raving, to show them that you have indeed been listening to them and that you are looking at the problem from their point of view. This is when we remember the 'satellites' that the individual threw out earlier. So the foreman might say to the man on the housing estate who lost his temper at the prospect of the power being turned off again: "You said you had a one-month old baby who you are worried about. If we run you a temporary supply...". Or "You said you were concerned about your mother. Tell me what I can do to help".

What we have just proved to them by this very simple interjection of information is that we have listened. Now, if this was one of the reasons that they believed that they had to shout and scream in the first place, we have removed the need for them to have to do it again, thus reducing the risk of escalation. If this encourages them to keep on talking, let them talk. The more information we have coming from them the better. Also it gets rid of any remaining pent up feelings, but in a now less threatening environment.

If appropriate, ask them to put themselves in your shoes too, especially if you know that you cannot fully meet their needs or demands. Even if you can't provide what they really want, ensure you offer alternatives, so that they feel they are getting at least something. Also, the act of choosing gives the person the impression that they are in control – and we all need to feel we have a measure of control. So, if the person wants action now (and that's impossible), we might say: "I'm sorry we can't do it now (for whatever reason) but we can do it on Tuesday or Thursday next week. Which would suit you better?" Or "We can give you an appointment to come to the clinic next Wednesday. Or someone could visit you at your home the week after that. What do you think's best for you?" The offering of a choice also creates the impression that there is no question but that the offer will be accepted.

When offering choices, *move away*. Walk to a window or out of the room or back to your van, or just turn away as if to attend to something else, if none of those is possible. The idea is that the individual feels free to decide without pressure. When ordering a meal, it is most unsettling to have a waiter hovering around. We want to take our time, not be rushed. That is important when reaching resolutions to problems too. It is a common courtesy that costs nothing and yields much.

If we know that what we will be able to offer is not substantial, it may help us if we set up an expectation of that in advance. "Look, the chances are that the manager won't agree to this. Is there anything else I can do for you if that happens?" Or "I'll talk to my boss but he may well say no. I'll come back to you in 15 minutes." When you come back in 15 minutes and say: "Well, I've been on the phone with my boss and he says no but how would you like (such and such alternative)?", the hearer is already mentally more attuned to not getting his way and therefore more open to other options.

The technique of delayed compliance can be useful too. This is where the benefits of a course of action are set out in advance and a person is given time to think about them. So a man apprehended with the bottle of scotch outside a shop might, could, when he has calmed down, be told by the security guard: "We know you've got the bottle. We can't let you go. I'm going to talk to my manager and if he calls the police, which I think he will, they'll arrest and search you. If you have the bottle, they'll prosecute. If you hand the bottle over now, it will look better for you in court". The security guard then goes to talk to his boss, leaving others to look after the shoplifter. By the time he returns, announcing that, yes, the police will be called, the shoplifter may have decided it is wiser to hand over the bottle than resist any more.

Remember, however, whatever stage of the negotiations you have reached, if the person starts becoming hostile and aggressive once more, you have to abandon all that, and go back to calming procedures and listening. Only when peace is restored can you successfully proceed with negotiations once more.

Praise and recognition

Two other important things to consider in this final stage are recognition and praise. If someone complies with you or works with you, thank them. We all like to be treated as though we are special. However, in today's society we all seem to be expected to go that much further without any degree of thanks. I can remember the value of praise when as a 16-year-old naval recruit I was given the task of painting the skirting boards of the chief petty officers' mess. It was a thankless task but I was eager to please, so I worked hard without a break to ensure that I did a good job. However, the longer I worked the more disillusioned I became with my chore. People were walking past me as though I didn't exist, and at times the odd huff from a passing chief petty officer even made me feel as though I was in the way – even though it was their mess I was painting for them. It was hard to stay enthusiastic when detailed to such a boring and repetitive chore and this was compounded by the fact that I didn't feel very welcome at all.

Then suddenly another chief petty officer appeared. He was obviously very senior and had been in the navy a long time. He came up to me and stood beside me. To young recruits such people were gods incarnate; we feared them. He then said: "I've been watching you, son. You've been at that job without a break all morning and, in spite of the fact that painting skirting boards is not mentally demanding, you've put a great deal of effort into doing it well. Now stop work for the day, go back to your mess, get cleaned up and be back here by five o'clock." I thanked him and at five minutes to five I was back at the chiefs' mess. I didn't know what I'd be doing, probably washing glasses behind the bar or some other meaningless or thankless task. Worst of all, I'd have no one to speak to, as chiefs didn't speak to recruits.

Then the old and bold chief appeared. "Come in, son," he said, and ushered me into the bar area. In the bar were about a dozen chief petty officers having a pre-dinner beer. "Right, listen in, you lot," said the old and bold chief. "This young lad has been painting our mess and he has made a sterling effort . He has worked all day without a break and not one of you has spoken to him, let alone offered him a drink. So, to make up for your ignorance, I have invited him as my guest for this evening. I don't expect him to pay for a drink all evening."

With that I was made very welcome indeed. I spent the whole evening in that mess and I had a great time, being told countless stories of the frightening and funny experiences of these senior men. From then on I'd have died for that man, the old and bold chief, and once I very nearly did. That, for me, was the value of praise and recognition.

1 Tehrani, N (1998). Debriefing: a safe way to defuse emotion? *The Therapist*, 5, 3, 24-29.

ENDNOTE

TIME DOES not stand still. Like individuals, organisations either grow or die, quite simply because organisations are made up of individuals. Therefore, if we want our organisations to grow, we must encourage growth in our staff – not just in numbers but in ability and, more specifically, in their ability to cope with whatever they face in their working day.

For a number of years now stress has been defined as something that is harmful. But, as we have seen, stress in itself is not a bad thing; it is the inability to cope with stress that does the damage. Without stress we would not be able to get up in the morning. The inability to deal with the challenges we meet at work costs us dearly. 'Stress' costs us as a nation somewhere in the region of seven to nine billion pounds per year in high staff turnover, high absenteeism, occupational illness and lost productivity.

Surely it should be good practice (and good business sense) to prepare staff for the challenges that they are expected to meet on a daily basis. If managers fail them by not giving them the competence and the confidence to solve problems and produce results, yet discipline them should they fail, staff will soon learn not to make decisions. They will learn to become helpless.

To combat this, staff need to be trained to deal not only with the expected but also the unexpected. How else can we expect them to improvise or use their initiative? If managers fail to prepare people, they will be left with staff who feel that they have no control over the situations they find themselves in. As human beings we are a creative, risk taking species, and it is these very basic needs that need to be satisfied and nurtured to stimulate and increase our coping ability.

As a nation we are starting to learn that we cannot expect people to suffer at work merely for the sake of a pay cheque. So we must provide support with post-incident care and counselling. But have we ever stopped to consider that by our inability to prepare our people for the challenges at work we may be creating the very disempowerment that we provide support for? If we don't do something about it we will just produce more staff who need more counselling. It can be likened to turning our staff into alcoholics and then sending them to AA meetings.

Industry today desperately needs a more proactive approach towards preparing staff for the daily challenges that they are expected to encounter. There is an abundance of research which shows that those individuals who participate in exercises that put them under pressure or risk live longer and cope better. It has been shown that people become more creative, productive, and efficient after such constructive pressure exercises. One eminent researcher even argues that risk exercise is so important that it should be encouraged and supported. And, interestingly enough, the Health and Safety Practitioner survey found that 55 per cent of respondents agreed that 'stress' needed to be introduced into the workplace in order to act as a motivating force.[1]

No one has the right to place anyone at risk and remove their right to safety by paying them a salary. However, every day we allow this to happen. The 'customer first' culture is producing a new breed of employee who not only feels isolated and unsupported in the workplace, but who is more fearful of being disciplined by the organisation than of being assaulted by a 'customer'. Yet, even for the good organisations who do care for their staff, the new 'American style' lawsuits keep popping up. 'No win no fee' solicitors are now everywhere. The fear of legal action is fast becoming a reality and people are using the writ like never before. If this cultural slide gets out of hand we are all doomed to a life where every act will be one of anxious anticipation – yet sadly the need for such action is justified.

Where staff are being injured due to an employer's negligence (or indeed belligerence) this route of redress provides individuals with a means to fight back. There are huge numbers of managers out there who understand all too well the risks that their staff take to make the system work. And as long as the system is working and no one is seriously injured, they will turn a blind eye to the irregular, and in some cases, dangerous and illegal practices that are being used. Yet, should someone be seriously injured, or even die, then questions will be raised by the very people who know all too well what is happening and why. For what purpose? To cover their backs – and in some cases this means that their backs are covered at the expense of the very staff who make an unworkable system work.

In the week that I left the Prison Service a young man committed suicide in his cell. He had tied one end of a ligature around his neck and the other on to the cell bars of his window. When he was found by staff he was already dead. When the alarm bell was raised I was only a few yards away from this particular unit and I attended immediately. I was the first officer on scene, after the two young officers who had found him. As you can well imagine, both of these lads were in a state of shock. Almost immediately other staff arrived, so I quickly ushered the two officers away from the scene. My concern was for them. Sadly nothing could be done for the young lad who had killed himself, in spite of the valiant attempts by staff to revive him. When the air ambulance arrived he was too far gone to revive, and the sight of a young life wasted in this manner, coupled with the indignity of his lying there, stripped naked while paramedics inserted tubes into him, was a very sad one.

When the two officers concerned had eventually regained some of their composure, anger started to set in. They had been warning management for some time about the risks on their wing. They were short staffed and the inmate population was rising. They were also very concerned. Had they done everything they could, and did they miss something earlier on in the day? These were the questions now being raised between themselves. Earlier that morning one of them had been talking to the young lad and he seemed in fine spirits. Had he failed to read the signs? Hindsight was now becoming a torturer.

A day after the incident everyone who was involved was called to a meeting in the boardroom to discuss the situation and its effect on those staff who attended. The anger and sadness was all too evident in my colleagues. One very senior principal officer who attended broke down and cried. To add insult to injury, however, we were joined in this meeting by a number of Prison Service psychologists, none of whom had attended the actual scene. They sat in a group opposite everyone else and began, in a very clinical manner, taking notes of the conversation and the points and issues raised by staff who had attended. Why exactly they were there was never made clear. One of my good friends, who had arrived on the scene immediately after me and had tried resuscitating the dead lad, was, like me, not too impressed by the attendance of this group of psychologists. "It was as if they were putting us in boxes, categorising us," he said. And that was the impression of us all, I'm sad to say. Due to the way in particular that this prison treated its staff, there was no trust between staff and management. Even in a tragic situation such as this, staff still feel that they have to be careful of what they say for fear of incrimination.

The point I'm making is that staff in many organisations make an unworkable system work and, when the system fails, staff are disciplined. Sometimes they even die. In many cases, it is for nothing more than doing their job in difficult and pressured conditions.

The vast majority of violent crime is committed by people who do not have mental health problems. Yet it is the very system in place for dealing with and caring for the mentally ill that creates risks that could be avoided. More than 50 people have been murdered by people with mental illness since 1993. The tragic case of Jenny Morrison, mentioned earlier, showed yet again that although 'statistically' the chance of being murdered by someone with a mental illness is low, given the correct circumstances it will occur. Unnecessary risks are being taken at this very moment by staff who still continue to place themselves at risk for a system that has failed them.

This is not to say, however, that some staff do not abuse their authority. They do. The question is why. I believe it is very often due to constant frustration, humiliation, perceived injustices, and threats which may all be part of daily routine. We have customer first strategies coming out of the woodwork, promoting a customer first attitude at, in many cases, the expense of staff. I have said it earlier in this book and I'll say it again here. There is one rule of thumb. If we look after our staff, they will look after the customers. Companies must stop investing in customers and start investing in staff. They are the best sales aid there is, but they need to feel valued, they need to be encouraged and they need to grow.

Just as it takes more facial muscles to create a frown than to smile, so many organisations spend more time telling staff what they cannot do than empowering them to achieve. Eventually the smile dies and is replaced by a permanent frown. Then the frown starts to take over the body. The lips become tighter, the eyes lose their sparkle and the frown is replaced by a glare. The shoulders slump, the walk becomes a shuffle, the individual believes that the world is against him – and no one wants to know.

Our organisations are only as effective as the people in them. I have offered in these last few chapters quite a number of strategies for reducing the risk that violence will result from angry confrontation. But it is not about tips and tricks. It is about a whole process of understanding where other people are coming from, and their needs as human beings. Empathy and understanding will get us all much further than slavishly following any how-to manual. Techniques are important; knowledge is vital. But so is fellow human feeling and respect, in every form it takes.

1 *Killing the messenger: the pathologising of the stress response* (1998). Strex Ltd.